The Politics of Historic Districts

The Politics of Historic Districts

A Primer for Grassroots Preservation

WILLIAM E. SCHMICKLE

ALTAMIRA
PRESS

A Division of
ROWMAN & LITTLEFIELD PUBLISHERS, INC.
Lanham • New York • Toronto • Plymouth, UK

AltaMira Press
A division of Rowman & Littlefield Publishers, Inc.
A wholly owned subsidiary of
The Rowman & Littlefield Publishing Group, Inc.
4501 Forbes Boulevard, Suite 200
Lanham, MD 20706
www.altamirapress.com

Estover Road
Plymouth PL6 7PY
United Kingdom

British Library Cataloguing in Publication Information Available

Library of Congress Cataloguing-in-Publication Data

Schmickle, William Edgar, 1946–
    The politics of historic districts : a primer for grassroots preservation /
William E. Schmickle.
      p. cm.
    ISBN-13: 978-0-7591-0755-7 (cloth : alk. paper)
    ISBN-10: 0-7591-0755-6 (cloth : alk. paper)
    ISBN-13: 978-0-7591-0756-4 (pbk. : alk. paper)
    ISBN-10: 0-7591-0756-4 (pbk. : alk. paper)
      1. City planning—United States—Citizen participation. 2. Historic
preservation—United States—Political aspects. 3. Historic districts—
United States—Planning. 4. Politics and culture—United States. I. Title.

HT167.S263 2006
307.1'2160973—dc22   2006015237

Printed in the United States of America

⊗™ The paper used in this publication meets the minimum requirements
of American National Standard for Information Sciences—Permanence of
Paper for Printed Library Materials, ANSI/NISO Z39.48-1992.

Contents

Acknowledgments

I want to thank Mitch Allen for suggesting I write this primer for AltaMira Press and Chris Anzalone, Claire Rojaczer, and Marian Haggard for seeing it through to completion.

The practical experiences that inform my opinions are indelibly linked to folks who've shared my political foxholes. Jim and Ann White, Frank Whitaker, R. N. "Buster" Linville, and Kaye Graybeal, this is your book as much as mine. I am also deeply appreciative of all the other friends and neighbors back in North Carolina, too numerous to name here, who made our Oak Ridge historic district campaign a success and spurred my interest in preservation politics.

I've been blessed with supportive friends in Annapolis who've helped me develop my thoughts. Greg Stiverson, Sharon Kennedy, Karen Theimer-Brown, Bob Agee, Patricia Blick, Jeff Horseman, Richard Bierce, Donna Hole, Rob Zuchelli, Don Deline, and Scott Whipple—thank you for your support and inspiration.

Myrick Howard of Preservation North Carolina first encouraged my political interest in historic districting. Pratt Cassity's booklet for the National Trust, *Maintaining Community Character: How to Establish a Local Historic District,* influenced my thinking in the early stages of evaluating the place of politics in the process. I am indebted to both.

Book writing is a family affair. Everyone close endures an author. My wife has been a selflessly encouraging and wonderful partner in this undertaking. So, Charlotte, I dedicate this book to you with love. My sons, Andy and Greg, have always borne up good-naturedly under their father's enthusiasms. You all make my world worth preserving.

Introduction: What D'ya Know?

Not much, you?

—opening of Michael Feldman's radio show,
What D'ya Know?

Isn't that the way it goes? You start a project and when it's finished you say, "If I'd only known then what I know now. . . ."

MY START

Some years ago I stood in front of a North Carolina Department of Transportation survey map hanging in the gym of the Oak Ridge Elementary School. Sketched on it was a highway improvement plan that would devastate our old crossroads community.

The proposal surprised my neighbors, too. Several spoke in the whispers of the already defeated. One said it was a "done deal." Another said you can't fight DOT.

But there was another fellow there, a Guilford County planner. He quietly told me that Oak Ridge could gain clout if we became the county's first rural historic district. I took his business card like a drowning man grabs a straw.

I spread the word. Soon a few of us were driving down to the county offices. It was the last moment of real peace we'd enjoy for two years. If we'd only known then. . . .

DO YOU KNOW WHAT I DIDN'T KNOW THEN?

What do you know about local historic districts? I knew next to nothing back then, not even the difference between *federally* designated and *locally* designated districts. So I also didn't know that local districts are the ones with teeth in them—the ability to enforce compliance as part of the local zoning code.

So I still had to learn that the most typical form of local designation is the *overlay district*. That's where the district is superimposed over existing zoning without affecting underlying permitted property uses. You might run into other forms from time to time, like separate use districts that replace existing zoning, but not in this book. We'll be talking about overlay districts. Here's a rough working definition of a local district: it is a defined area of historically, visually, or culturally related properties that is designated and administered by a city or county government to preserve the community's identifying character. But a definition can take us only so far. We need to add that:

- District ordinances derive their authority from state and federal enabling legislation.
- All district properties are designated as contributing or non-contributing, though work done on all of them is subject to regulation.

- Historic districts are typically administered by an officially appointed Historic Preservation Commission (by that or some similar name).
- HPCs issue Certificates of Approval (also termed Appropriateness) as part of the local permitting process.

Not knowing that, I knew nothing about getting a district designated. I just assumed we'd ask the County Commission to approve ours. You see, I didn't know that:

- A district has to meet criteria for certifying its historic significance and integrity.
- Designation typically involves due process hearings before the HPC, Planning Commission, and the City Council or County Commission.
- The process can take many months, even a year or more, to complete.

And I didn't know all hell would break loose when we took the plan to our neighbors.

I found that attitudes toward districting cut across all lines— political, economic, gender, ethnic, educational, or what have you. Any national statistics on preferences simply dissolve into individual personalities at the local level. Some folks you know will be just great. Some will break your heart if you let them.

On the up side, I had no idea how many fine people I'd meet in the preservation community. Local preservation groups pitched in, as did the statewide nonprofit group, Preservation North Carolina, and our State Historic Preservation Office. The National Trust for Historic Preservation and the National Alliance of Preservation Commissions (NAPC) were invaluable resources.

INTRODUCTION

WHY A POLITICAL PRIMER?

They all helped us learn what we didn't know about preservation. They taught us *what to say*.

But *how to win*, there was the problem. We got bits and pieces of political advice, all of it good, yet nothing systematic. I was intrigued by how little other folks actually thought about politics when politics was what they were doing every day.

Still, I never imagined that one day I'd be writing this primer on the politics of running a districting campaign. Yet here it is. Each chapter is a brief treatment of an often complex topic. I've designed the layout and content for nonexperts like you and your next-door neighbor who need to know how to act to win.

Others will help you with the more specialized preservation component of your effort. Some might disagree with the primacy I give to politics. As my friend Sonia Schmerl has reminded me, people tend to get interested in preservation for reasons other than politics. (What?! There's something else?) Well, whatever your interest, my purpose is to get you to think *politically* about each step along the way before you act *politically* for *political* success. The others will get the point when you win.

So, tell me now, as you step out to win your district's designation: What do you know about preservation politics? If your answer is "not much," then this book is for you.

ONE

Before You Take Another Step

History may not always repeat itself, but it sure tends to rhyme.

—Thomas Boswell, sportswriter, *Washington Post*

So you're a local civic activist and you want to start a historic district. It's a great idea, but not an easy one to carry out. Are you hesitant about stepping forward, wondering how to begin without getting off on the wrong foot?

If you are, I have a simple answer. Do nothing until you get comfortable with the idea that for the foreseeable future you're going to be doing politics more than preservation.

That's obvious, isn't it? You yourself can't create the historic district. All you can really do is start the designation process rolling. If you work the politics of the process right and stick with it, you might end up with a district that looks like the one you have in mind. Most likely at this point you're not even clear about what you want.

Well, you're not alone and you no longer have to rediscover the wheel. Others have gone before you, and Tom Boswell sums up my assumption in writing this book: that although each historic district is unique, there are still enough similarities in those experiences to permit some general observations that may help you think more clearly, and effectively, about what you do.

Your basic story line has played out again and again across America. Local activists propose a historic district. An opposition arises. A rancorous community debate ensues. A divided city council or board of commissioners looks for a way out. Usually an up or down vote settles the question. Sometimes, like in Newnan, Georgia, a compromise is struck that strings out hope beyond reason.

LOST CHANCES

"We could have been the best of the small towns," Newnan's Georgia Shapiro says.[1] You might know her town. It's where *Fried Green Tomatoes* and *I'll Fly Away* were filmed. But to hear her tell it, what's happening to Newnan's first historic district brings to mind another Southern movie, *Dead Man Walking*.

"Every day is a danger," Shapiro says. She refers to the City Council's last-minute decision in 2003 to set up voluntary design guidelines instead of the proposed historic district with mandatory review and compliance. The City's planning staff suggested the change as a compromise. Realists on both sides of the issue know it's largely an empty gesture. The ordinance affords no dependable protection, even from a property owner bent on mischief. Newnan's historic properties are living on borrowed time, trusting in luck for a daily reprieve from the inevitable.

Now I'll bet that's not what you wish for your own community. Yet it's not an isolated event. From Palo Alto to Staten Island, elected officials often react coolly to the notion that communities with historic resources need the shelter of enforceable law.

Why would they think that way? Well, I can think of any number of likely motives. But for starters, I think that at a very basic level, your average local legacy just doesn't look like important history to many of them.

Let's call it the George Washington syndrome. I'll lay you odds that once you start your districting campaign some opponent at a public hearing will complain, "Why is my property historic? George Washington didn't sleep there!" It's amazing how many people think such a lame line is brilliant analysis.

My guess is that every place George slept is either gone or somehow already protected. Certainly our most cherished historic communities, like Boston, Philadelphia, Annapolis, and Charleston, have successful districts already in place. In fact, the fifty states share more than 2,000 historic districts at this writing. Some places are chockablock with them. Chicago alone has thirty, Phoenix twelve, Boulder eight. Yet there are but twelve in all of Arkansas. There's plenty of room for more. In fact, we preservationists will never run out of places to nominate because our definition of what is historic is ever changing.

One reason is that what is new sooner or later becomes old and may acquire historic significance. A presidential bedroom is no longer needed to justify interest, nor is a Frank Lloyd Wright design. A Michigan preservationist argues that while Hartland Township hasn't a single important structure, taken as a whole it's historic. But what does that signify? Opponents charge that we've sacrificed any meaningful definition of historic to a sacred cult of the merely old. Like it or not, it's a view that has political punch. As Mayor Bill Welch of State College, Pennsylvania, said when he vetoed the city's preservation ordinance in 2002, "When everything is historic, nothing is historic."[2] Unless George Washington slept around in your neighborhood, you've got your work cut out for you.

ALTERNATIVE FUTURES

So what's a preservationist to do? Quite a bit, actually, as you'll see in the following chapters. But while we're here, let me try to get you to look at this from another angle.

As the case for outright *historic* preservation has become increasingly difficult to make stick, we've actually shifted much of our talk over to the role that districts can play in the kinds of *futures* we prefer. Preservation of the past has become strikingly forward-looking.

It's a kind of good news, bad news perspective. The bad news is that it blurs the difference between us and other groups fighting over such hot-button topics as urban housing teardowns—where land is worth more than the homes on them—and big box retail stores in formerly rural communities.

The good news is that this strategy is something politicians can understand. Their eyes may glaze over when you mention ambience, character, a sense of place, an intangible heritage, or cultural landscapes. But you speak their language when you bring up property values, economic vitality, tax bases, mixed-use development, managing sprawl, and securing a wide array of other measurable benefits.

Local planners talk enthusiastically about preservation taking its place among other public efforts to influence the types and rates of change. "Preservation law can be a powerful development tool," says Lisa Bennett of Batavia MainStreet in Illinois.[3] This makes for a powerful political argument, too, so much so that some of us make a point of talking as much as possible about economic development instead of historic resources.

Lisa Selin Davis has a vision of Tempe, Arizona: "It could be known as a city with charming historic districts and well-preserved neighborhoods embracing a profitable revitalized downtown."[4] If you thrilled to the first part, you're a good preservationist. If you sat up straighter at the ending, you're already thinking politically, too.

PLAYING THE GAME

There is a downside, of course. Historic districts that are designated for any number of economic and social advantages may in fact have little to do with genuine preservation. Sometimes it's just preservation as decoration. Other times, it's not even that.

My wife, Charlotte, and I recently drove 8,000 miles from coast to coast looking at historic districts. Some, like Santa Fe, were truly remarkable. Some unfortunately looked like they had never seen a design guideline, voluntary or not. If the local town council is trying to entice travelers to the bric-a-brac shops and alternative café at Broad and Elm, why worry about front porches on Third Street? Sometimes you just keep on driving.

Even in our least successful communities, you can be sure that someone like you meant to do better. But historic districts are not creatures of pure preservation. They are political from the get-go. I don't mean the deck is stacked against preservationists, but that preservation gets shuffled together with all sorts of conflicting ideas, principles, and interests. Your historic district initiative gets you a seat at the table, but you don't get to deal the cards.

Which reminds me of something I learned on a Las Vegas stopover: If you want to preserve your resources, you'd better know how to play the game.

Our game is the politics of historic districts. Just like any other game politics has its own rules. They are largely impervious to our preferences, and you ignore them at your peril. If you think that's overly dramatic, I suggest you think again before you take another step.

NOTES

1. Kevin Duffy, "History a Matter of Heart in Newnan," www.ajc.com, *The Atlanta Constitution-Journal*, June 9, 2003.

2. William Welch, "Why I Vetoed the Historic District Ordinance," www.centredaily.com, *State College's Home Page*, September 9, 2002.

3. Jane Adler, "Preservation Haul," www.chicagotribune.com, *Chicago Tribune Online Edition*, December 28, 2003.

4. Lisa Selin Davis, "Historic Preservation: Finding Room for History in the Desert," www.Americancity.org, The Next American City, Inc., 2004.

TWO

Thinking Politically about Historic District Designation

You can't reorder the world by talking to it.

—Buckminster Fuller

Like Tip O'Neill's view of politics, all preservation is local—and nowhere more so than in the creation of a local historic district. From initiative to designation, the process is local. When the issue is in doubt, the process is also almost exclusively about local politics.

ON WINNING

Getting local designation under these conditions typically means winning a hard fought political contest. For every successful campaign, other deserving proposals fall short. It is only by winning that we are able to translate what we want into public policy.

Evidently that's not as obvious as it seems. Some preservationists deplore the imperative to win and the competitive strategy it implies. They prefer a path of educating for consensus, trusting in reasoned discourse and the final persuasiveness of their vision. I think this approach has advantages, but it's hardly ever enough.

It is precisely because the historic district will benefit your community that you have a moral responsibility to win. *The worst thing in politics is to be right and to lose.*

ON PRESERVATION ADVOCACY AND POLITICS

When we win political battles for historic districting, it isn't simply because we're right on the issues or because our cause is just. The political landscape is littered with the bones of just causes. We win by outmaneuvering our opponents.

When we fail, it's often because we've confused issues with politics, overemphasizing *policy* relative to *politics* in the policymaking process. We anticipate a designation process driven by preservation issues, only to find that policy considerations are but one—and not clearly the most important—factor in the political calculations that determine the outcome.

Politicians are happy to use our arguments for preservation, or those of our opponents against it, as cover for the positions they may end up taking for such political reasons as public opinion, ideology, party discipline, and political ambition. Their own personalities and subjective biases may also deflect an issues-focused agenda. At best, policy issues are the *input*, and politics the *process* in public decision making. To mistake the one for the other is like confusing grain with the gristmill.

National, state, and local preservation organizations have done an outstanding job of supporting citizen activists who typically spearhead the toughest historic districting campaigns. District proponents are time after time the best-informed party in the local *policy* debate. So how is it that we are often outmaneuvered in the *political contest*?

If you attend a preservation conference or two it's hard not to get a sneaking suspicion that many preservationists think that "politics" is what other people do. Other people, you know, like developers. And preservationists sometimes wear their difference like a badge of honor.

When these preservationists are forced into politics by what they call "challenges to preservation" (as if preservation, not change, were the norm), they like to dress up *their* politics as "advocacy." Consider the session titled "Advocacy: An Advanced Guide" offered at the National Trust's 2003 National Preservation Conference in Denver. The blurb advertising it stated, "Successful advocacy for historic preservation is as diverse as the resources it strives to protect."

Not quite. If every preservation fight were that unique, what could we possibly learn from studying them? Battles won by heroic effort would simply pass into Homeric tales told around conference tables—or maybe just abbreviated into the "inspiring three-minute success stories" previewed for a Denver luncheon.

I see it differently. Preservation campaigns are indeed very different when we're looking at *what* things are to be preserved—a public space, a working-class housing tract, a waterfront commercial district—and *why* our communities should protect each one. That's what I think of as *advocacy*.

But when we look at *how* we as activists actually win decisions to save these resources—at what makes us successful—we find that the dynamics of what we *do* are essentially the same from case to case. Now that's *politics*.

When advocacy and politics are made to travel together, politics takes a back seat. The moderator of a roundtable at the 2004 meeting of the NAPC in Indianapolis recognized a questioner who asked about politics. He stopped still, looked around the room, said "Ohhh . . . *pol*-i-tics!" and quickly changed the subject. And so it goes, more often than I can tell you.

NO FAULT ZONE

So who's to blame? No one, really.

Politics is a natural activity, but it is hardly pleasant. It speaks a harsh language of power and interest. Wanting to avoid it is a healthy impulse.

Most of us prefer to orient our lives toward other pursuits—and our communities are better off for it. The proper study of preservationists is preservation, just as it is the law for lawyers, wealth for economists, and faith for ministers. If they all thought first in terms of politics, what a dreary and luckless world this would be! So, it's right and proper for preservationists to hew to what they know best: our historical, architectural, and cultural legacy.

Still, local activists need real political help. The preservation community may think it's giving it, but often it isn't.

Why? Because avoiding politics is one thing. Responding to it in ways that suit us rather than politics' own requirements is something else altogether.

We can't very well advise the uninitiated on preservation politics if we don't squarely address politics ourselves. I think we'd all be far better off if we simply broke politics out from under the cover of advocacy and gave it the attention it's due on its own.

ON POLITICAL THINKING

Let's face it: advocacy just won't do for politics. When push comes to shove in the political arena, local activists are the ones who sup-

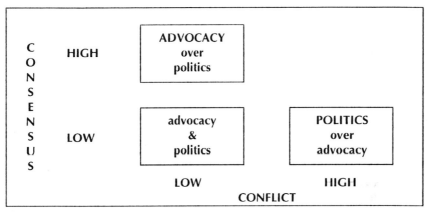

Figure 2.1
Where the degree of consensus among interests in a district is high (vertical axis), advocacy will
be more important than politics in securing designation. Where conflict is high among interests
(horizontal axis), politics will play the critical role.

ply the victories that the rest of us like to cheer. So don't you think
it's time we paid more attention to supply-side preservation?

The best way to start is at the beginning with Politics 101.

Politics—any politics, not just preservation politics—arises where
interests come into conflict. Basically two things can happen. One,
the parties share enough common ground to resolve their differences
and reach agreement. Two, where agreement isn't possible, politics
decides the issue by a vote that favors one party over the other. Advocacy, by which I will now mean *persuasive education*, plays a different kind of role in each scenario, as represented in figure 2.1.

In the first, where conflict is low and agreement is possible, politics is mild background noise. Here the preservation specialist—
with the aid of an experienced mediator—may nudge differing interests toward final consensus by educating the parties to the merits
of preservation on a case by case basis. In this high consensus/low
politics setting, much hangs on the advocate's technical excellence
in framing the argument and getting the message out.

But as conflict among competing interests escalates, the prospect
for mediated consensus fades and advocacy is downgraded to a

supporting role. In the high-intensity world of many preservation battles, the activist must take dead aim at winning the vote for designation, whether or not this involves changing people's opinions by reasoned argument. Politics at this level values strategic thinking and tactical agility over technical expertise, and excellence is known by winning.

The difference becomes obvious in a hotly contested campaign to designate a historic district:

- Going in, you'd better be superbly briefed as an advocate on all your preservation talking points: what designation does, what the law is, why the district deserves protection, and so forth.
- Yet it is possible to know all this and still enter the fray as the *best informed* but *least prepared* participant—unless you yourself are politically astute enough to grasp the flow of the political contest on your own.

This is why learning to think politically about preservation *now* will be critical your success *later*.

Preservation politics is about assuring we have an advantage over our opponents when we need it. Advocacy always plays the leading role in defining and nurturing worthy ends for the community. But it can't substitute its own standards and methods, which aim at specific preservation outcomes, for the fluid expectations of competitive politics.

Where conflict over districting remains unbridgeable, the political process—at its best—aims at balancing our interests against those of our adversaries. Exactly where this balance is struck when the votes are cast is settled by the relative influence each party brings to bear on the moment of decision. Our job is to see to it that our interests are heard by decision makers and that our influence prevails.

ON LEARNING FROM EXPERIENCE

The political problems of district designation are reborn with each new local campaign. Every new effort repeats the experiences of the others, within a fairly limited range of variations in the roles played by elected officials, property owners, consultants, public administrators, the media, and private sector associations.

Each designation campaign will have its own peculiar features. But time and again, experience shows that the main dimensions of the process are both regular and predictable. The political dynamics that can be distilled and taught include:

- Mastering the political process.
- Planning and strategy.
- Campaign organizing and the qualities of leadership.
- Framing a practical vision.
- Anticipating and handling the opposition.
- Conducting community meetings.
- Managing issues, petitions, and public opinion.
- Dealing with public officials.
- Strategizing for public hearings.
- Winning the vote for district designation.

From a strictly preservationist point of view, politics is rarely satisfying. Yet the principles you advocate as a preservationist will be judged politically in the long run by your ability to apply them to practical effect in advancing your community's welfare.

The problem is that the way most of us first get involved in preservation just about assures our coming late to political sensibility. So now I want us to cast our thoughts back to beginnings so that we may find our way forward, as Plutarch said, "like watermen who look astern while they row ahead."

THREE

How It Starts

I guess it's time you heard our story.

—Humphrey Bogart, *Passage to Marseille*

Thousands of local preservationists just like you have been baptized by fire. They haven't become preservationists because they're architects, historians, city planners, lawyers, professors of fine arts. They've joined our ranks because they have found value in the legacy of some local property that they have fought very hard to preserve.

In this fight, they have experienced politics in the trenches. They have done battle all along a learning curve from reasoned arguments to adversarial gamesmanship to backdoor politicking. Some have won. Too many have lost. Others are fighting still.

Of course, not everyone's challenge has been so daunting. Some districting has begun under fairly auspicious circumstances. Sometimes the local government has sponsored the plan. Other times the social situation is settled and the district becomes a public celebration of civic pride.

But often preservationists-in-the-making don't get interested in politics until they find themselves in the middle of a high-stakes contest among conflicting interests. They're behind in the game and pressed for time. So like the ever-late White Rabbit they hasten to make up the deficit. Upset by the course of events that has brought them to this pass, they often fail to understand their place in the process.

How about you? Wherever you are, and whatever the peculiarities of your situation, I think you'll find something instructive in the generic tale I have to offer.

JUMPING INTO POLITICS ...

We preservationists have an unusual ability to make a personal connection with property we don't own. "The second my husband and I started driving up and down these streets," Paula Soest says in Orange, California, "I just fell in love with the whole thing."[1] We tend to infuse places—from open farmland to old town centers—with significance because those places have taken on meaning and value in our own lives. Thus is New Orleans' French Quarter described as "the physical essence of who we are."[2]

Some of us come to believe that the time-softened places we hold close are special and somehow safely apart from areas that have been touched and spoiled by others. So when the hand of change falls upon us, it seems to come out of the blue. The more sensitive we are, the more we express "shock" and "outrage" at what for others is a commonplace occurrence. We seek a political solution. Sometimes it begins to take the form of getting a historic district designated.

I suspect you're like most Americans who are fortunate enough not to have to think about politics on a daily basis. So you probably think that because the political process is receptive to your claims, the process somehow begins when you get involved.

The truth is that politics is a continuously flowing river. When you step into it for the first time the experience is new only to you. Usually by the time you and I get involved, the political process of change has been going on for a long, long time.

Developers—to pick one group, for the sake of a story line, whose actions trigger historic districting campaigns—are different. As Baltimore preservationist Brad Rogers observes, they think in terms of markets and ordinances, not meaning and value. By the time their project comes to light, they have typically invested much time—perhaps years—and borrowed money to negotiate sales with property owners, to conduct market studies, and to get zoning ordinances changed at those boring commission meetings no one else much attended. ("I'd rather watch grass grow," a friend confides.) With these land use and other major matters well behind them, they are locked into the project personally, emotionally, and financially.

It's just then, when the developers are eager to finalize such details as deed transfer and construction permits, that you want to be heard. More than that, you actually want to start the whole discussion over again. Of course, you don't want to talk about just the project at hand. You want to get back to basics. Basics like, what is truly good for the community and how does it relate to the built environment?

Out of this comes your proposal for district designation. This is the moment when you're most vulnerable. Smart opponents will jump on your plan as a desperate reaction—an afterthought devoid of real, compelling, intrinsic merit.

. . . AND SKIPPING OUT AGAIN

Can you blame the developers for being exasperated? As one critic reasonably charges, preservationists who come late to the game "shirk responsibility. [They] do not plan ahead, but wait until new construction nears and then cry for government to intervene."[3]

You and I might think that we act courageously by speaking up, but a critic in Manitou Springs, Colorado, sees it as indicative of a deteriorating social character: "Something's changed in the last 20 years," he says, "we've kind of become a society that goes to City Hall to solve its problems."[4]

I'm not so sure it's all that new a phenomenon. Who among us hasn't said at some time or other, "There ought to be a law!"? Asking for help with grievances is at least as old as representative government itself.

Yet our high regard for public opinion polls does seem to reflect a contemporary belief that elected officials ought to do whatever we tell them, instead of using their own judgment colored though it may be by their interests and values. So if we want politics to be about preservation, then, by golly, it will be if we insist upon it. Let's go down to City Hall and demand what "we the people" want.

Then, too, we're sometimes less likely to turn to local officials for relief than to blame them and the "system" as accomplices in unwelcome change. Dale Rahn, founding president of Orange's Old Towne Preservation Association in California, says of his group's beginnings: "Those early years were acrimonious to the established power structures in the city, but with new ideas and a far more creative vision, we persevered."[5]

Does any of this sound familiar? Don't we all, when we step up to act, behave as if preservation were too important to leave to politics-as-usual?

If you've said yes, then we've got a problem. Do you see what's happened?

The "you" of our story has come late to politics. You've entered politics only wanting to change politics. You hardly got your feet wet in the river of politics-as-it-actually-is before you skipped out again. From their place in the real, continuing flow of political events your opponents can't help but feel a bit like the hit-and-run victim who reported, "An invisible car came out of nowhere, hit me, and disappeared."

So be careful. We can become so intoxicated with our vision of a well-preserved community that we can't see straight when politics intrudes on our reverie. If that's the case, then we're going to make the cardinal mistake of thinking that preservation is one thing and politics something else—an incompatible and inferior interloper. "Mere politics," a Philadelphia preservationist calls it, hoping his city's heritage won't be dragged down by it. A Boise activist sees her situation similarly. "It's a very emotional issue for us," she says. "We need to get the politics under control and do what's best for our future."[6]

How do you see politics? Here's a quick self-test: What's your first reaction to the West Coast preservationist who writes of his cause, "Let's see if politics can be removed from the issue and let it become a black and white issue of 'is there enough evidence to nominate the district by itself.'"[7] If you said "uh-oh" when you read that, then you're on the right track.

A REALITY CHECK

Isn't it obvious that politics doesn't interfere with preservation so much as we force preservation onto local politics? When we go to politics to enact our districting legislation, it's politics that sets the rules, not preservation.

We have some nerve, then, when we confront politics as it actually is with an abstract ideal of how we think it ought to be. That's why finding out how the political process actually works can be a sobering experience.

NOTES

1. Michelle Gringeri-Brown, "Inside Preservation: A Grassroots Effort Pays Off," *American Bungalow Magazine*, www.americanbungalow magazine.com, 2002.

2. Christopher Tidmore, "New Orleans and the Charleston Experiment," www.itsonlypolitics.com, August 20, 2003.

3. Rex Curry, rexy.net, n.d.

4. John Dicker, "Preservation or Coercion? Manitou's Historic District Polarizes Property Owners," www.csindy.com, i-News, October 3–9, 2002.

5. www.opta.org, Olde Towne Preservation Association, n.d.

6. Emily Simnitt, "Boise OKs Historic District," www.idahostatesman .com, *Idaho Statesman*, June 1, 2004.

7. www.mkhelp.com, July, 1998.

FOUR

A Walk through the Designation Process

"Why," said the Dodo, "the best way to explain it is to do it."

—Lewis Carroll, *Alice in Wonderland*

When you were in school, did you enjoy the lesson on how a legislative bill becomes a law? Yeah, me neither.

Few things can kill an enthusiasm for politics as quickly as an organizational chart of local governmental operations. So instead of going through a "the-head-bone-is-connected-to-the-neck-bone" exercise until our sit-down bone gets numb, let me walk you through a simulated, quite typical real-life experience.

The facts in our simulation won't match up precisely with yours. Not to worry. Being good at politics isn't mainly about facts. Facts change over time and they differ from place to place. You'll need to find out the specific process in your own community. But good questions about how political processes work and how to win are everywhere the same, and they're always in fashion.

An exercise like ours, which is driven by questions and leading statements, can serve as an imaginative bridge between where you are at the start and where you need to go with designation. At the very least it should help to demystify City Hall.

A SOUTHERN DIALOGUE

Come along with me now as we travel to the lovely port city of Wilmington, North Carolina. We're going to walk into City Hall just as if the only thing we know about historic districts is that we want one. I've picked Wilmington because of Kaye Graybeal. In the early 1990s, Kaye was our consultant in Oak Ridge, North Carolina. She soon became Wilmington's preservation planner—the position that Maggie O'Conner now holds—and today Kaye serves as planning manager.

I've arranged for us to meet with Kaye and Maggie in Kaye's top-floor office. The room with its conference table to one side looks as I had expected, knowing Kaye. It's bright, well-organized, and efficient. Preservation and community service awards fill one wall. The large window looks out to the Cape Fear River in the distance.

What follows is a slightly edited version of an unrehearsed and unscripted hour-long conversation among the three of us. Oh, yes . . . and my neighborhood community is fictional.

Me: It's a pleasure to meet you, Maggie. Thanks for joining us. How familiar are ya'll with old Alopecia Shores out toward Bald Head Island? Our historic area is receding alarmingly and we think district designation could help. What can we do?

Kaye: The first thing we should do is check to see if your neighborhood has already been surveyed and qualified for the National Register under previous grant studies.

Me: But all we want is a local district. And anyway someone's told me that a National Register district doesn't have any teeth, but a local district does.

Kaye: That's right. But if it has already qualified for the National Register we can assume it qualifies as a local district. But if it hasn't, we'll have to start from scratch.

Me: What do you mean "qualify"? We're one of the oldest beach communities around.

Kaye: Yes, but you're asking for a new zoning overlay for the district that will basically regulate its design features but not the use of properties. The HPC will need documentation that it's worthy according to criteria set by state enabling legislation and our local preservation ordinance. National Register criteria track along the same lines. From the HPC to the Planning Commission to the City Council, everyone has to be able to point to documented evidence.

Me: Why so many steps? What's so difficult?

Kaye: Every city or county has its own procedures guided by state enabling legislation. Most of them, unless they're very small, have at least one advisory commission that handles technicalities and makes recommendations based on their expertise. They're made up of citizen volunteers who are charged with the responsibility for getting a well-prepared proposal to the final decision makers—the elected officials.

Me: I see. So what if we haven't been surveyed?

Kaye: Then we'll have to decide whether we can budget for a consultant to do the study next fiscal year. Or you as a neighborhood might want to raise the money to pay to have it done. That would be quicker.

Me: Would the City decide to fund this because they want us to have the district?

Kaye: I think we should first send you back to Alopecia to get a feel for the degree of support. We can't just take *your* word for it. [Smiles.]

Maggie: When we go to the City Council we need a lot of people saying "yes, yes, yes"—more than say "no, no, no." Even if you pay for the study, you'll still need support, because politics is involved. If you don't ask people to join early on, their feelings get hurt, and they're against it because they don't know why they're excluded and they don't understand the regulations.

Kaye: And that it's done behind their backs, or it's a plot. So you have to talk about the benefits, get people excited. . . .

Maggie: But even one person can get things started. That's why we went ahead today and met with you. The main thing you need to know is what a district is and why you want it.

Me: OK. So who down here makes the decision to budget for the study?

Kaye: If we think the project looks feasible, we'd ask the City Council to approve a budget enhancement in our consultant line item. We could just ask for funding "for historic designation survey and report." Then we would use it for your neighborhood if there appears to be interest and support. That would avoid asking the Council specifically about your neighborhood before we're ready to go ahead with designation.

Me: So we wouldn't have to go down to the Council to get them to give you the money?

Kaye: You could, but that could be too much too soon.

Me: That's good because we worry that as soon as word gets out about our proposal, people will start fighting it without knowing what it's about. When you ask for a show of support, isn't this biasing the process by giving early warning to our opponents?

Kaye: You'll have to go to the community with a public meeting before the report comes out, to inform them about the possibility. You might show them a vague or broad boundary with a disclaimer that it could change.

Maggie: You might want many community meetings. The first one would be for information: what it means to be in a historic district, what's going to happen, the positive benefits of it. And the drawbacks.

Kaye: But don't label them drawbacks. We say, "Here are some things you need to consider to decide whether the process will benefit you."

Me: So we have a community meeting, you get the funding, and the study is favorable. Whose proposal is this now—yours or ours?

Kaye: It would be a staff proposal if the City paid for the study, with a recommendation of approval to the HPC, the Planning Commission, and the City Council.

Me: Who has control over the details of the proposal? For example, can we leave out property owned by die-hard opponents?

Kaye: Zoning laws don't promote "Swiss cheese" holes in the district. That could be considered illegal spot rezoning. What you'll have is an overlay district on top of underlying zoning, and the district has to be made up of contiguous properties. But you could leave out properties on the periphery. It would be a judgment call. That's where politics enters in, depending on how strong you think support will be for what you want.

Me: If we do that won't we be open to charges of gerrymandering?

Maggie: You don't want to leave properties out just because of present owners. Properties change hands. This is where you have a community meeting, to bring people around. You've got time to work on them.

Me: How long? We'd like to get it done yesterday!

Kaye: Maybe a year, more or less, after funding the survey. There's the study, and the time needed for it depends on scheduling and the district's complexity. We'll send the completed report for comments from SHPO. [She pronounces it "SHiPO," the State Historic Preservation Office. Every state has one, by one name or another, pursuant to the federal National Historic Preservation Act of 1966.] They have the opportunity to speak to the integrity of the proposed district. Then if you look at just the formal meetings, it'll take one month for the HPC, one for the Planning Commission, and one for the City Council to review it, if all goes smoothly. If it doesn't, any of them could continue their deliberations longer, send the proposal back for more study, or ask for more information.

Me: How much does the City Council pay attention to SHPO?

Kaye: They need something to hang their hat on if they are going to vote in favor of something that some citizens are going to oppose. They can at least say, "Well, the State says it's very worthy." I think sometimes decision makers don't necessarily trust the Preservation Commission, so if the HPC can add credibility to the proposal by saying that SHPO approves, they'll have a stronger case.

Me: Why wouldn't they trust the HPC?

Kaye: It depends on who's in office—maybe a property rights advocate—and who's on the HPC—a few zealous commissioners can make the entire HPC appear unreasonable.

Me: What if SHPO isn't fully supportive? Will we have to redo the report?

Kaye: Yes. Or we can go forward and make a case for doing something locally that SHPO doesn't agree with, if we feel we have the support for it.

Me: Who's the "we"? Who's going to make those kinds of decisions? We in Alopecia Shores or you downtown here?

Kaye: It's a partnership. If the City has paid for the survey report and the planning staff is bringing it forward to Council, the staff will work with the community even if some people are likely to stand up and object. It's a subjective call for us, though the technical merit of the proposal is objectively defensible. At some point staff has to make the decision: Can we lend this support, is this a proposal that most people are behind? If we have broad consensus, we can take it forward while acknowledging there are people against it. Because we're making the recommendation, we have to be confident that the proposal meets our zoning regulations and is something that can be politically supported.

Me: When you write the proposal, are you going to run it by us for our opinions? What about our opponents?

Kaye: We'll make sure everybody, including opponents, can obtain a draft copy either here or online, or we'll pass it out at public meetings.

Me: Will you amend it just to suit the opponents?

Kaye: No, it's still a partnership with you, with the whole community. If we find out there are people extremely opposed to parts of it then we would need to assess whether we need to bring it back to the community to get consensus or whether we've done all we can and take it on to the commissions and the City Council.

Me: But once people state their positions, isn't it hard to change them?

Maggie: I think you're wrong. People listen and change. Some may become strong supporters. They need to understand what it means to be in a historic district—what you can do and what you can't do, and that's when you talk about the design guidelines.

Me: What guidelines?

Kaye: Once you are designated, the HPC will apply design guidelines in evaluating applications for certificates of approval for work projects in the district.

Me: When do we write the guidelines—or do you do that?

Kaye: Unless there is something really special about some aspect in your district, the guidelines that the HPC already uses in other districts will apply to you. But we don't want a lot of conflicting norms out there among the districts—we have five already. That would complicate the HPC's work and maybe opening us up to legal challenges.

Me: So we can't really negotiate much on the content of the guidelines.

Kaye: Maybe a little, but not really much. If you were the first district, you'd have a lot more flexibility. But here, you'll probably just want to explain the guidelines very clearly so people don't think they're more of a burden than they actually are.

Me: Is it right to say you'll be handling the official process with boards and commissions downtown and it's up to us to handle things in Alopecia Shores?

Kaye: Once staff gives the proposal to the HPC and the HPC supports it, the HPC will be the petitioner of record who asks for Planning Commission support and final Council approval. You will be able to testify at each stage and so will your opponents. How that goes depends on what you've accomplished in your neighborhood.

Me: What exactly is the Planning Commission's role compared to the HPC's?

Kaye: The HPC verifies that the proposal is justified in preservation terms. The Planning Commission—because the district will be a zoning overlay—considers how the proposal conforms to zoning code and whether it conflicts with other City interests and plans. The City Council looks at anything at all that it thinks is important.

Me: What if the Planning Commission says no?

Kaye: The HPC can decide to appeal the decision to the City Council.

Maggie: That's why you need community involvement. You don't want to just leave it up to a consultant or us or the HPC. You want to show it's about community pride.

Kaye: And you have to find all the intersecting interests in the community that will support you.

Me: So will you be on our side?

Kaye: What we do as staff is present the technical merits of the case. We act as advisers to the Council. We have to know what Council members like—what their interests are—but we are also trying to do what's right for the community. When I was in Maggie's job I once asked, "Can I be an advocate in presenting this proposal? I *am* the preservation planner." My supervisor, who had the job I have now, said I didn't have to be just neutral and technical. That's a judgment call, too. As staff, you have to realize that you're going to be criticized by the district's opponents, and Council members might see staff as trying to ram something through that people don't like. You have to be careful about the degree of advocacy and passion that you show. If you can present the case so that it's undeniably worthy of historic designation, then you don't have to espouse all the other benefits of preservation. Just show that it meets all legal requirements for merit. That's best. If you do that, you've done your job as staff.

Me: How about the City Manager's role in this?

Kaye: The City Manager is at the top of the City's administrative hierarchy. The City Manager is the Planning Director's boss and the Planning Director is the Preservation Planner's boss. The City Manager would be informed by subordinates about the plan and might oppose it for any number of reasons and stop it. It's up to staff to persuade everybody right on up the administrative line, including the City Attorney.

Me: Would we as citizens lobby the City Manager if there were resistance to the district?

Kaye: You can ask for an appointment with the Manager or you can go to the City Council. The Council is the voice for the citizens in City affairs and can tell the Manager that citizens should be allowed to pursue their initiative. But if we do our job as staff that shouldn't be a problem.

Me: What about the Mayor? Will you talk with the Mayor or should we?

Kaye: Staff won't be talking to the Mayor. That's the job of the City Manager. The Planning Director might suggest a meeting with the Mayor, department heads, and staff. It's a good idea to get the Mayor onboard before going to the City Council.

Me: Is there anything else that can be done to improve our prospects with the Council?

Kaye: We could request a work session with the Council to educate them—tell them, here's what people think the pros and cons are. We'd tell them how staff has addressed those concerns. Citizens can attend this type of session to listen, but not speak. Then we could summarize this presentation in the public hearing.

Me: How would you handle the benefits side?

Kaye: We could use case studies from other communities, with hard numbers to support economic arguments, for example. We could say we've seen it work in other places, so we think it could work here. So you try to back up an opinion or a recommendation about a particular benefit with evidence on here's why or here's how it has worked someplace else.

Me: I'm uneasy about the community meetings. We're not preservation experts. Should we coordinate with you and have you speak for us?

Kaye: From experience, that could be a problem for staff to meet with advocates ahead of time. We'll come and talk about what a historic district is and what it'll mean to your community. But it's your meeting and you'll be the ones to convince your neighbors.

Me: Maybe we need our own preservationist to advise us.

Kaye: You could hire your own consultant, even if the City does the survey study. Or you could contact SHPO. They keep a list of qualified consultants. You can also invite SHPO to come to a meeting. Also think about inviting such private sector organizations as Preservation North Carolina or Historic Wilmington Foundation.

Me: Do we need an attorney?

Maggie: When you go to the HPC or the Planning Commission with an attorney it sets up this other world. Everybody suddenly gets very tense, very careful about what they say. People stop working together, and you need people to want the district.

Me: So what do you think we have to do next?

Maggie: You have to have a plan. But what you do depends on how you read who's sitting on the City Council, because some politicians may be leaning more heavily toward preservation while others aren't. So what kinds of risks you can take in the campaign depends on Council members. You might have a very favorable Council when you get there, and the opposition won't matter. But you could have a Council that doesn't want to approve it, and every single supporter will be important to you.

Kaye: That's when you talk about economic development, creating a protected investment environment, and other benefits. You need as many people from the community pushing their interests with you as you can get together. You need to know the people you'll be working with in the community and on the City Council.

Maggie: And you need patience. . . .

On that calming note, I thanked them for their time and assistance. By the time I had crossed back over the Cape Fear, I was already seeing implications for planning and strategy rising to the surface.

FIVE

On Planning and Strategy

You gotta convince me that you know what this is all about, that you aren't just fiddling around hoping it'll all ... come out right in the end!

—Humphrey Bogart, *The Maltese Falcon*

We got a friendly reception in Wilmington, didn't we? If you're not that lucky in your first encounter with local government, well, it's good to be put on notice sooner rather than later.

So what did we learn? That when you take your districting idea to City Hall, what you see is what you get. You need to see things as they are, not as you think they should be. What we'll be saying about City Hall applies to county offices, too.

YOUR STATUTORY SETTING

So let's take care of first things first. Pick up the phone, call City Hall. Ask to speak to a planning official and make an appointment

to meet face-to-face. While you're on the phone get yes or no answers to the following basic questions:

- Does the City have a *preservation ordinance* that provides for
  local historic districts and specifies the designation process?
- Has the City put in place a *historic preservation commission—*
  by that or any other name—charged with design review and
  designation responsibilities?
- Are there *design guidelines* in place that will apply to your
  historic district?
- Does your City Planning Department have a *preservation
  specialist* or at least someone conversant with preservation
  concepts and legislation on staff?

Just as soon as you can, get copies of the ordinance and guidelines—if there are any—to read before you go in for a chat. This will
save time and make you a more intelligent listener. We could've
been better prepared for Kaye and Maggie, don't you think?

But what if there is no ordinance where you live and you have
to start from scratch? That's just a complication—an obstacle, not
a barrier.

In fact, demonstrating support for districting might just be
what it takes to get an ordinance passed and a HPC set up. The
Huntington Woods, Michigan, City Commission created its Historic District Commission in 2003 for the express purpose of
studying a districting proposal.

In such cases, we—and I mean you and all the folks in and out
of government who'll be working on the project—don't have to
come up with an ordinance and HPC design entirely on our own.

Every state government has preservation statutes on the books
to guide us. We at the local level will be able to decide a good many
particulars. But anything the City does will have to conform to state
legislation governing the establishment of districts and HPCs. To

find out more about your state's statutory framework, contact your State Historic Preservation Office.

So keep that appointment downtown. Find out how your local designation process really works, what falls to you to instigate and what kind of people you'll have to work with.

Don't hesitate. "Questions," cinema sleuth Charlie Chan once said, "are keys to door of truth." Ferret out where your input can make a difference *and* where you shouldn't tread. Bear in mind that when "no" means "no" for a good reason, that's a good answer too.

The more you know the less likely you are to think, say, or do foolish things.

LOCAL PROCEDURAL DIFFERENCES

Did you notice that Kaye and Maggie didn't start by asking us what we wanted them to do? They just laid out the planning procedure mandated in Wilmington and told us what they could do in terms of:

1. Budgeting for a study.
2. Surveying district properties and preparing a map.
3. Getting the City administration onboard.
4. Developing the draft proposal.
5. Getting SHPO evaluation and comments.
6. Submitting the proposal for HPC review and recommendation.
7. Submitting the proposal for Planning Commission review and recommendation.
8. Submitting the proposal for City Council consideration and vote.

This is exactly what we needed to hear. We could plan on it—if we were pursuing a district *in their town*.

What about in yours? Municipalities seem to enjoy coming up with their own ways of doing things. Take Urbana, Illinois, Rockville, Maryland, and Detroit, for example. Each has a differently arranged designation process that mixes in pretty much the same ingredients. You may find some differences, too, if you're in the minority of cities that have a "strong mayor" system, where the mayor acts as an executive and has veto power. Most, however, have mayors who are members of their city councils.

So get with a planner and map out the way it's done in your town. I want to assure you, though, that no matter how different your flowchart might look, the politics that courses through it will be the same whether you're from Urbana, Rockville, Detroit, or Anywhere, USA.

We'll be using Wilmington as our model town because its process is common, simple, and straightforward. Once you know what you're facing, you'll need to make mental adjustments to adapt what we say here for your own purposes as you plan your campaign.

ON PLANNING

But you know what? The more you think about it the more confusing the very idea of a *plan* becomes.

Follow me for a moment: Let's say we've gone ahead and developed a plan that's tailored to our own town's designation process. But what is it we actually *do* with the plan? Well, we implement it, of course. But what does *that* mean and how does it work to get us what we want? How should we *conceptualize* the process to make sure we're in control of what happens?

Should we think that implementing a plan is like assembling a jigsaw puzzle? You know what I mean. We've got all the pieces sorted out and lined up. Now all we have to do is to lay hold of each one and fit it into place, moving from success to success, until the puzzle is completed. Is that it?

If that's the plan, then we're in trouble because we really haven't accounted yet for politics. A *plan* is just a plan until it comes up against competing interests. That's when we need a *strategy* for handling our opposition and winning over the decision makers.

So what's holding us back? Well, I think maybe we just don't want to fight with our neighbors. It's not a pleasant experience. So we delay.

On the other hand, we're encouraged in our procrastinating by the very way the formal designation process works. It's clear, though, that we can't duck politics forever. And just like with any protected enterprise, the longer we put off facing up to our competition the more perilous our position becomes.

THE DESCENT INTO POLITICS

The first few stages in the Wilmington model deal almost exclusively with preservation matters right up through the HPC hearing, pushing politics to the sidelines. After that we'll find ourselves on a steady descent into the much more politically complexioned worlds of the Planning Commission and elected officials.

In the best of all worlds, as Kaye and Maggie suggested, our case for districting would be so inherently persuasive that advocacy could work its magic and designation would be a snap. Once in awhile it actually works that way, but you can't count on it.

The hard political truth is that those who sit on the City Council are free to ignore every staff and commission recommendation that crosses their desks. Planning staff are employees, and commissioners are no more than citizen advisers to the Council in the policymaking process. Their support is an advantage, no doubt about it. But it's in no way predictive or binding on the City Council.

Their recommendations carry no more authority than individual Council members are inclined to give them.

What's your Council's record? Unless it has a proven track record of deferring to the HPC, I'd advise you to prepare for the worst.

If you walk into the Council chamber with nothing more than a solid proposal, staff support, and a couple of advisory commission recommendations, then all bets are off. You may have done everything by the book, hit all your procedural marks, satisfied every legal and technical prerequisite for designation, and still lose the final vote. In fact, your Council members may actually say they agree with every argument you make for districting *and still refuse to do what you ask.*

So *what* can we do about it? And *when* should we do it? These are strategic, not planning questions.

ON STRATEGY

Do you remember Kaye's offer of a partnership with us? It captures our strategic challenge brilliantly.

Look at the list of procedural steps again. They involve us, and yet there's *nothing there that you and I are personally required to do.* If we wanted to—that is, if we were truly allergic to politics—we could just leave everything to the planning staff and the HPC and hope for the best. But hope is not a political virtue, and planning staff need our help as much as we need theirs.

If you take a closer look you'll see that there are actually *two* processes running on converging tracks toward designation.

- The first is the formal procedure that runs its decreed course from the resources study to designation.
- The other is much more informal and political, and it's our particular contribution to the effort.

This second, strategic line of action begins back in our home district. That's where we lay the political groundwork for the proposal's favorable reception before the HPC, Planning Commission, and City Council.

Think of it this way. Both of the tracks we've sketched out lead toward winning designation. In one, we do what is required. In the other, we do what it takes. They are twinned and pulled together like the two sides of a zipper.

Nothing we contribute on our track is mandated, but we are well advised to think of our role in terms of:

1. Initiating the process.
2. Influencing the study.
3. Holding community meetings.
4. Carrying out a petition drive.
5. Managing a media campaign.
6. Testifying before the HPC.
7. Testifying before the Planning Commission.
8. Lobbying and testifying before the City Council.

No single one of these tasks is ever complete in itself, and everything we do bears consequences for every following action. If we mishandle any one, our mistake will have rippling effects all the way on down the line.

Yet even our successes can't insure us against reversals. No single accomplishment is ever certain until the final vote is taken. Even momentum has no loyalty.

That's why politics is more like a game of chess than a jigsaw puzzle. With a jigsaw puzzle you know when you've made a good fit, you know that the piece will stay put, and you know you can build confidently upon it. But in chess, as in politics, the game changes with every move. You can never know for certain that any move is the right one because you can never be sure how the other player will react.

A political strategy is practical only if, like chess, it embraces fluidity, uncertainty, and only general predictability. We know just two things for certain: where we start and where we want to end up. After our first move, everything is tactical improvisation looking for advantage in swiftly moving events. But the long thread of our effort, what connects all from beginning to end, must be our sustained strategic effort to bend the course of events our way.

Chess grandmaster Savielly Tartakover once explained the difference between strategy and tactics. "The tactician," he said, "must know what to do whenever something needs doing; the strategist must know what to do when nothing needs doing."

So in the early going, while things are still moving our way in the formal process down at City Hall, that's the time for strategic preparation. The first thing we need to think about is what it means to build community support in what will certainly be a most difficult political climate.

SIX

Our Strategic Line: A Community in/within Conflict

The most basic decision in politics is whether to be conciliatory or aggressive.

—Dick Morris

We have seen how the district designation process works at City Hall. So what do you think our chances are with your neighbors? How should we approach them?

Should we be conciliatory going into our campaign, or is it better to be aggressive? Do you believe that we invite trouble by looking for it? Maybe you're wondering how we can know the limits of cooperation if we don't pour all our energies into working together. For that matter, how can we be confident of any strategy?

Hard to tell, isn't it? So what do we do, just pay our money and take our choice? In truth, I suspect that we don't want to commit one way or the other until we see how things play out. We expect that our opportunities will be a mixed bag anyway, don't we?

Let me suggest an approach that allows us to be as conciliatory or as aggressive as circumstances warrant. Let's take a strategic line that combines the underlying political reality of a *community in conflict* with the possibilities of nurturing a newly vital sense of *community in the midst of conflict*.

EDUCATED ILLUSIONS

First, though, I want to know whether you can handle conflict. The first time I made the case for winning through competitive politics a conference attendee accosted me. "I hear what you're saying," she said, "but I still feel that preservation is too important not to bring everyone along by educating them."

Educating them? You mean all they have to do is know what we know and they'll agree with us? Some, sure. But *all* of them, even *most* of them?

What a quaint notion. She's a perfect example of how we can get so deeply invested in preservation values that it distorts the way we see and interpret the once familiar world around us.

There was a time, I'm sure, when we were easy with neighbors who had views and aspirations of their own. Diversity was healthy, wasn't it? But maybe we think that's a luxury we can no longer afford. Now anything different from what we want is all too easily held to be rationally, aesthetically, even ethically suspect. We brand our adversaries with being unschooled, unsophisticated, antisocial, spiteful, selfish, greedy, or some other *slur d'jour*.

Such immoderation in our judgment can't help but inspire immodesty about our own place in politics and lead us to folly. We need to get a grip on ourselves. No one I know ever won over the majority we need by being a snob for the truth—especially when that truth isn't a gold-plated self-evident one.

INSTINCTIVE POLITICS

I think an editorial in the *Florida Quest* said it as well as anybody: "there's a natural instinct among many to resist being told what they can or can't do with their property."[1]

Private property rights are indeed a far more commanding *instinct* in American politics than preservation. And long ago, even Machiavelli—the master political manipulator—warned his powerful Renaissance prince that he could do just about anything he wished as long as he left other folk's property alone.

Have no illusions. Our opponents enjoy advantages that have little to do with being smart, and they instinctively seem to know which buttons to push to get other folks in a lather and send us up the wall.

Talk about an educational deficit! You'd think we'd know by now that politics runs more on emotion than intelligence. Didn't Sam Adams advise us long ago that people "are governed more by their feelings than by reason"?

So we've embarked on a political enterprise that is a great deal less thoughtful than we'd probably like it to be. We should expect that our ideas will be roughly treated by at least some neighbors.

A COMMUNITY IN CONFLICT

Much of the direct political conflict we'll encounter is just superficial and passing. Hostility and resentment are here today before the vote, gone tomorrow afterwards. But all of it springs from far deeper tensions among interests and feelings that are shaping—as they will continue to shape—our community.

These tensions simmer below the surface most of the time. They may bubble up here and there as specific projects—a new condominium block, demolition of a church—raise concerns. Once in awhile they come to a boil. No doubt our proposal will turn up the heat.

But the conflict that boils over into a community fight over designation doesn't begin with our initiative nor will it end with districting. The historic district will just be a different, and to our mind a more successful, way of dealing with it.

This elemental conflict is an inescapable fact of everyday life. That's why, when we think politically, we think in terms of a *community in conflict*.

A COMMUNITY WITHIN CONFLICT

Our focus on conflict doesn't stop us from working to alter the way people view preservation, even if their interests don't match ours. So part of thinking politically has to be devoted to community building, to molding individual attitudes and linking up diverse interests in support of preservation.

As we look around our neighborhood we should be scoping out how much room we have for invigorating *a larger sense of community within conflict*. Still, we know we're not going to win over everyone. Some of our neighbors will remain unmoved. Some will stand against us.

OUR DUAL STRATEGY

Taken together, these two perspectives frame what will be our two-part political mantra: *There is enough mutuality of interests to make a historic district possible, and enough conflict among interests to make it—and our designation campaign—necessary*. It's up to us to make our case on both counts and win the decision.

Our strategy, then, is straightforward. We will do what it takes to forge a broad coalition for districting wherever we can, and we will use that coalition to outpoint those who remain unalterably opposed to us.

In the process we will discover how much consensus is possible and how much conflict is unavoidable. This flexible approach gives the fullest practical play to our yearning for positive advocacy and consensus building while being thoroughly realistic about the practical requirements of political success.

In today's slang, we got game. Now let's go look at the field of play.

NOTE

1. Editorial, "Lake Helen's Historic District Changes Are Good," *Florida Quest*, September 14, 1998.

SEVEN

Makers, Breakers, Takers, and Shapers: The Political Field of Play

Who's on first?

—Abbott and Costello

What's on second base, I Don't Know is on third, and that's about as far as I can keep things straight in Abbott and Costello's hilarious baseball routine. Keeping the who's who of political players straight in your own districting campaign can be even more confusing.

At least in baseball you know the shape of the diamond and can put players on bases. But how should we diagram who's playing where on districting issues?

Do we sketch out left field and right field, who is liberal or conservative, Democrat or Republican? From where I sit, I think that's looking too far out into the haze of general tendencies to be of any real use. Better we pull back to the infield where we can clearly see that everyone's primary interest—whether in baseball or in preservation—is in real estate.

Home plate is the most valuable piece of property in baseball. The whole game is organized and played around that central fact. And so it is with preservation. You have to focus on people's primary interest in real estate to keep your head in the game.

WHO'S WHO?

So let's start identifying who's who politically by making real estate our base organizing concept. Our most important question, then, isn't who's for or against preservation. Not even close. The most important thing we need to know is who owns the properties we're going to include in the district.

Note: who *owns*, not *occupies*. When you send out notifications and announcements, you don't want them tossed out by some renter or leaseholder you *think* is the owner.

Every overlooked property owner—whether they live in the district or out of state—is a political and public relations strike against you. We just can't afford to lose support from mistakes.

Ownership creates an exclusive group of interested individuals. Others who live or work in the district have a right to express their opinions, but when it comes to districting, the City Council will *first* weigh heads and *then* count them. You'll find that the heads that count the most are the ones that voice the weighty interests of property owners.

Property interests, of course, aren't monolithic. And because those interests are not all the same, politicians aren't going to treat them all equally, either. Perceptions in both quarters—those of property owners and the policy makers—are nuanced by any number of considerations, such as:

- Whether properties are owner occupied, owned by local voters, or owned by absentee landlords with few ties to the community.

- Whether properties are used for residential, commercial, institutional, governmental, agricultural, or other purposes.
- Whether owners are private individuals, corporations, not-for-profit institutions, or public governmental authorities.

These differences can create tensions among *groups* of property owners. The College Hill district in Greensboro, North Carolina, has running conflicts because of its mix of family residences, a YMCA, a commercial strip, fraternity and other student housing, churches, and bars. But *individual owners*, too, will keep a skeptical eye on neighbors like themselves, ever watchful of their own particular interests.

Each owner, then, will approach historic districting through a different, carefully guarded perspective that passes through the lens of his or her own self-interests. But no matter how different they are, their attitudes will always be fundamentally different from those folks who don't own property in the district.

This won't keep property owners from working with non-property owners. Yet the difference still runs like a fault line between them.

So the first thing you want to do is get yourself down to City Hall, go to the tax and property records, get hold of the property maps covering the district, and start answering these questions for each parcel of land:

1. Who is the owner of record?
2. Who pays the property taxes?
3. Is the owner local? (Record contact information.)
4. Is the owner an individual, or is it a corporate, governmental, or other entity?
5. How is the property used: residential, commercial, institutional, governmental, agricultural, mixed use, etc.?
6. Is the property itself owner-occupied, rented, leased, or vacant?

Record each parcel's acreage, if it's available, in case you need it later.

Don't assume that the City can just give you accurate lists. If you want it done right, do it yourself. You'll never have to say, "That's not what they told me." That just makes you sound careless.

Precision is your byword. Activists in the Bungalow Heaven Landmark District in Pasadena, California, could attest to 962 lots and the inaccuracies of some public records. Now create usable lists of information from what you've found:

- List owners who live in the district in their own residences.
- List owners who work in the district in their own premises.
- List those who own investment properties for rent or lease.
- Make separate lists of properties by type of ownership: private individual, corporate, governmental, private institutional, etc.
- Make separate lists of owners by how their properties are used.
- Group properties under the individual names of owners who hold title to more than one parcel.

Your goal is to be the unimpeachable master of facts and details so you won't get caught making unsubstantiated claims.

As you work, you'll detect emerging patterns of mutual interests among your neighbors that are almost certain to be clearer to you than to the owners themselves. That's because few folks ever lift their vision beyond the immediate setting of their own properties— meaning that an understanding of their interests in districting needs, quite literally, to be mapped out.

WHO'S WHERE?

So let's do some mapping. You should be able to get a copy of the official tax map showing all the built features of the district's physical landscape and how they're zoned. Make sure your copy is big enough—blueprint size is perfect—for marking up individual properties.

Start by boldly outlining the district. Then denote all structures and features that contribute to the historic significance of the district. If you don't yet have a historic resources survey, then estimate them now and make changes later.

Next, devise a consistent legend for other group identifications. I'd suggest using a mix of transparent color markers that you may overwrite, colored pens, colored adhesive dots, and written abbreviations. Look at all properties, *both contributing and noncontributing*, and do the following:

- With transparent markers, color code each property by use: residential, business, private institutional, governmental, or other, including mixed-use.
- Identify properties that are owner-occupied.
- Identify properties by type of ownership: private individual, corporate, governmental, private institutional, etc.
- Draw lines to connect or encircle multiple properties owned in common and identify the owner.
- Indicate all properties that you believe are currently vulnerable.

Check with your Planning Department for a rundown of rezoning, building, or demolition applications as well as any preliminary inquiries that might affect district properties. You have a right to anything that has entered the public domain. Highlight the more important concerns, but mark even innocuous things on the map.

Property owners will also be influenced by developments immediately adjacent to the district. And owners just outside may be motivated to support or oppose designation depending on its spillover effects on them.

Now go find out what's important to your neighbors in the district. Talk *with* them, not just *to* them. But don't let them in on the district idea just yet. You don't want folks talking until you've made your first community presentation, as we'll see in chapter 14.

Has anything happened recently to agitate them? Are there any new issues on the horizon, like a school or hospital expansion, a road widening or cell phone tower? Is the quality of residential life under pressure in one particular quarter? How about economic decline among retailers?

Are there any issues in the district that pit one set of property interests against others, such as tearing down residences for church expansion? They needn't be so specific, either. General problems often percolate along lines where different property uses run alongside one another, as where a commercial sector abuts residences. List key issues in the map's margin and connect them by arrows or lassos to specific locations on the map.

Now sit back and look at your map. Don't just focus on problem spots. Where are the less marked up, quiet areas in the district? Owners in a well-maintained, especially affluent, neighborhood will be a tough crowd to motivate.

WHO'S WHAT?

Whether people back us or not will have little to do with their personal political views. Liberal Democrats can be just as prickly about property as conservative Republicans. Yet both will readily back districting if they see it's in their interest.

The usual left–right political labels don't really explain much. I'd like you instead to think of property owners in the district in terms of makers, breakers, and takers:[1]

- *Makers* (that's us) have the vision, resources, and leadership qualities needed for bringing a historic district into being. We are convinced that our valued property and related interests are best secured by district designation. This in turn, we'll affirm, promotes the common good of our community.
- *Breakers* are inclined against districting from the start, and they have the resources to mount an effective opposition against us. They tend to find disadvantage for their interests under designation and are unresponsive to appeals to civic virtue. Breakers must be persuaded, co-opted, neutralized, blunted, or defeated.
- *Takers* are unconvinced but persuadable property owners. More or less satisfied with the status quo, and often having limited resources and interests, they don't yet see where the district will make much of a difference to them. They can't get excited about the district, yet they're not especially motivated to oppose it either. In the end, they'll pretty much take whatever happens in stride.

Takers straddle the line between our most ardent opponents and us, and they typically outnumber both. They are our main political interest, not the breakers. Our key strategic challenge is not to beat our opposition in a head-to-head contest. It is, rather, to isolate its most adamant elements—those who will not let themselves be persuaded, cajoled, or enticed—on the extreme edge of opinion and so split them off from our more moderate doubters as we move to win the middle ground.

Non-property owners aren't going to choose sides unless they're fairly invested one way or another. Because they don't own property, few of them will have any real influence outside of group associations unless they have personal political influence.

Any number of organizations, however, may have a broad membership including both property and non-property owners who share ideas and interests—but not property—in common. So we can add to our taxonomy of property owners:

- **Shapers**, who act as individuals or associations, *independently of property status*, to influence the outcome of our districting campaign. They may act alone or in cooperation with makers or breakers, who may already be members of their associations.

Shapers may be local, state, or national preservation organizations, property rights groups, tenants' and merchants' associations, a regional development board, the tourism industry, cultural heritage and political action groups, behind-the-scenes operators at City Hall, your local board of realtors, developers, architects and contractors, newspapers, and anyone else able to exert influence on public opinion and the political process.

These relationships may be diagrammed as follows:

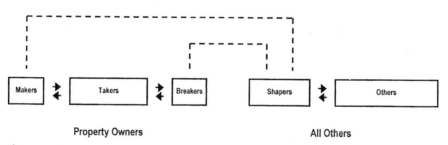

Property Owners   **All Others**

Figure 7.1
Individuals are distinguished by their relationship to district real estate: some own property, the rest do not. All owners are divided into three groups, and shapers are distinguished from other non-property owners who take no interest in districting. Arrows indicate individuals shifting between groups as they change their minds during the districting process. Dotted lines represent support or cooperation between shapers and makers or breakers.

LEVEL GROUND

We have explored the political inequities of property ownership. We've walked the district and found differing interests. We have split up the players into separate and competing classifications, and we've begun to think about the strategic implications of what we've found.

And yet in one area all the active participants—makers, breakers, and shapers—stand on common ground and share the same objective. They all seek to maximize their relative influence in the political process.

By thinking this way, we are able to treat all parties with equanimity. We know that they must act under the same political compulsions that govern us. We know that this basic fact is unaffected by property status, by personal animosities, by appeals to sentiment or principles, by professed ideologies or attributed motives.

This level-eyed reading of the lay of the land is an advantage. We see our opponents' true interest in politics possibly even better than they see it themselves. We can anticipate their best efforts and capitalize on less. Our own campaign, then, gains focus and economy of effort. And we ourselves gain clarity, and confidence for the game ahead.

NOTE

1. Stephen D. Krasner first suggested these shorthand label terms to describe state actors in the construction of international economic systems. I have redefined them to suit our purposes.

EIGHT

Leadership and Organization

You go to war with the army you have, not the army you want.

—Donald Rumsfeld

You're it, ready or not. You're the face of historic preservation in your community, or you will be soon. Next time you look in the mirror, think "Who else ought to be in this picture?"

Effective leaders build effective leadership teams. Whether you're starting from scratch or within an established organization, the first thing you have to do is put together a campaign steering committee.

THE STEERING COMMITTEE

Shaping public opinion is like working in wet cement. Think like the audiences you want to influence. The first time your neighbors come to a community meeting, who should they see waiting for them? Who will inspire them? Who will give them the confidence that when they side with you they're doing the right thing?

You can't do it all by yourself. One person can make a difference, but not the whole difference. The history of many districts is written in the biographies of individuals with indomitable wills, such as that of St. Clair Wright, who saved Annapolis, or a special vision, like John Gaw Meem's for Santa Fe. But you can be sure that, to a person, they've known how to use the talents of others.

Reaching out to others doesn't mean pulling everyone in. The steering committee you want is a small, closely knit group of capable people who can work well together.

By small, I mean no more than can fit around a good-size kitchen table—and just that informal. You'll have a mountain of technical material to master, a multiphased process to attend to, and a neighborhood campaign to mount—all under the pressure of closing deadlines.

You few will have to have each other's confidence that agreed-to tasks will be done right and on time. No excuses, no pettiness, and no hurt feelings, please. Check your egos at the door. Take advice, share responsibility, and create an atmosphere of no-fault leadership within the circle. And since you're going to be scheming to win, what goes on in the group has to stay inside the group.

CHOOSING YOUR LEADERS

So who do you pick for the team? Select them with these criteria in mind:

1. *Intelligence.* Everyone is going to have to be a quick study, with an ability to analyze problems and draw conclusions.

You don't want the group dragging anchor in muddy thinking. Clarity is essential to crisp decision making.

2. *Personal Character.* Members must want to do the right thing, not just win arguments. Their public face should be one of integrity, dignity, and good humor.

3. *Discipline.* Tolerate no loose cannons. Everyone must agree to defend every group decision. Opponents will exploit dissent. Exclude anyone who can't keep confidences.

4. *Commitment.* A meeting missed is a meeting lost. Even one person's absence steals time and effort from everyone. At least two members will have to find time during the occasional workday for taking care of business at City Hall or special events.

These four qualities alone won't add up to much without *enthusiasm* and *generosity*. You want people eager for success, folks who look forward to meetings, who will forget the lateness of the hour, and who will cheer each other on with a generous and forgiving spirit. If you can get such members, they will make up a whole greater than its parts. That will compensate for individual weaknesses.

THE CORE MEMBERS

Your *key decision makers* should be three to five members who own property and reside or work in the district. Anyone who doesn't own property has to be widely admired. You'll need:

- A torchbearer and lightning rod, a performer accustomed to public speaking and able to think in front of a not always friendly audience.

- A campaign manager for keeping the committee's work focused and on track.
- A member typical of the community's mainstream property owners.
- Members typical of other large constituent interests.

Because some property owners will likely see preservation as too "out there," make sure at least one member has a conservative occupational background. You want those people to think, "Hey, *they're* for it and they're OK, so it must be OK for me too."

Avoid flakes, whatever else you do. Some self-styled preservationists provide the best possible targets for opponents. Simply shun fanatics, eye-rollers, and folks with obvious ties to other divisive issues. We don't need that kind of baggage.

All other members can be outside advisers. I recommend three types.

1. A Preservation Specialist. Your committee needs expert advice. Ask your SHPO or local preservation organization for a list of qualified consultants. Professionals are worth the price, if you can afford it. If not, look for a university in your area that offers graduate degrees in preservation. An intern or a thesis writer will have all the energy and enthusiasm of a young professional on the rise.

Using the City's preservation planner has pluses and minuses. The upside is that the staffer knows local politics, too. But public servants aren't actually "yours." They serve the community at large, and your opponents will say their tax money is being used to oppose them. They'll say the City is conspiring with you before they've had a chance at due process. If things get hot, the Planning Department may back off and leave you hanging. Be aware, too, that whatever you say to staff is of legitimate interest to your opponents and may be in the public domain.

2. A Political Insider. Move heaven and earth to get someone who knows City Hall inside and out: who's who, who's interested in what, who's aligned with whom, who follows whom, and where the push-buttons and power levers are. You want someone who is political to their fingertips. A former official will do admirably.

Failing that, look for what I call a political "gym rat." The first time I met one—a jack-of-all-trades in the land development business—he was at a Council hearing, standing in the back, taking notes, whispering asides, chuckling, shaking his head. He would react to a quip, a ploy, a rejoinder, a close vote like a sports fan responds to a great play, a close call, a painful defeat. He could sense a shift in momentum, and he knew voting records like lifetime batting averages. He'd seen it all "a thousand times," he said, and everybody called him "Jim." Now that's the kind of guy you want to bring in for a briefing on how to win.

3. An Attorney. Districting adds to local zoning law, but you shouldn't need a lawyer unless the other side starts blowing legal smoke. There are several areas where knowledge of preservation law is indispensable:

- Credibly answering property owners' legal questions in community meetings.
- Explaining the constitutionality of historic districting.
- Correcting inaccuracies in references to the Fifth Amendment's "takings" clause.
- Riding herd on your City Attorney's legal counsel in hearings.

Be cautious about hiring a polished attorney to handle the burden of public speaking for you on other issues. You don't want to appear too uptown while presenting the case for districting back home. Get a lawyer who knows that a public hearing is not a courtroom.

YOUR LARGER ORGANIZATION

What do steering committees do? They plot the strategy and guide the campaign's course. They help a larger number of less involved but still important folks work together toward a common end.

Not every able seaman mans the bridge. There's more to running a successful campaign than making the key decisions. It's wonderful to be blessed with loads of volunteers who can work on publicity, serve as block captains, mobilize support for meetings, research public records, enter data, write supportive letters, lick envelopes, work their own contacts with policy makers and the media, help with documenting district resources, put together information packets, and do the many other things that need doing.

Effective leaders don't tell others what to do. They create conditions in which others are encouraged to do their best. Have your key leaders keep in touch with volunteers on a weekly basis. Once you're ready to take the campaign public, start holding meetings with them to reinforce their sense of value, to assure they're working together, and to improve ongoing planning.

There's a big difference between taking my advice on having a small steering committee, on the one hand, and turning away eager volunteers, on the other. Saying "no" to supporters who want to be part of the inner circle is simply impolitic.

It's better to work out a kind of affiliate status. Give them significant responsibilities and bring them in for regular talks. Who knows? You might find talents you hadn't suspected before.

WEBSITE CAMPAIGNING

The Internet is transforming grassroots politics. As "information central," a website enables us to spread our message with maximum content control while reducing the time, effort, and costs associated with traditional strategies. Other advantages include:

- Compressing our core message while providing click-throughs to more detailed pages and off-site resources.
- Keeping connected with supporters to assure their interest and loyalty.
- Recruiting and coordinating volunteers.
- Advertising events.
- Broadcasting alerts and responding to opposition attacks and misinformation.
- Facilitating e-mail messaging campaigns to influence officials.
- Improving coalition building with other groups and organizations.
- Providing easy media access to our campaign.

If you plan on using your site for fund-raising, be sure to incorporate your organization under 501(c)(3) IRS status.

A basic site may be managed by a high school student, though a professional operation is preferable. Our site should have the right look and feel for our community and be competitive with whatever our opponents put together.

Once you buy your domain name, put it on all your campaign literature. But remember that not everybody has Internet access. For many older or economically strapped folks, the Internet culture is still elitist and a political liability if you focus on it overmuch.

Keep the site simple and user friendly. But never think that a presence on the web can replace people working in the community.

Even then, no combination of mere mortals is ever ideal. Go with what you've got and work your contacts. There's a political village of more or less ready supporters at the local, state, and national levels. So let's turn now to how we might approach them.

NINE

Working with Shapers

Our friends show us what we can do, our enemies teach us what we must do.

—Goethe

What other friends can we count on in this fight? Who are the shapers—influential people or groups—who can help us win? What do you have to do to get them onboard?

Many folks have interests related to ours. Some want what we want. Others oppose what we oppose. But be cautious. It's often true that "the enemy of my enemy is my friend." Yet when you're both watching your adversary you're not always seeing eye-to-eye.

Once you identify potential partners with compatible records, how should you proceed? Do you just assume common cause and go in brimming with enthusiasm? Or will you find that you should have thought this through before you sat down at the table with them?

CHAPTER NINE

A SHAPER'S PERSPECTIVES

So let's go to the source and find out. I've asked Gregory Stiverson to talk with us. Greg is president and CEO of the Historic Annapolis Foundation (HAF), one of the premier local preservation organizations in the country.

Historic Annapolis, as it's also known, grew out of the preservation initiatives of St. Clair Wright in the 1950s and 1960s. Today it owns and operates several historic properties in the historic district and provides a wide array of preservation programs and services.

We're talking at my place, Flag House Inn, a Victorian bed and breakfast between the Naval Academy and the harbor just a crooked block from Greg's office in the Shiplap House, formerly one of Annapolis's earliest colonial taverns.

> **Me:** Welcome to Flag House, Greg. Let me set this up for you. Assume I've caught on fire about getting a new historic designated. Next thing I'm in your office—or the office of someone like you in another town. I just know you'll personally want to do everything you can to help us. Would I be right?
>
> **Greg:** Well, a great deal depends on where my organization—the one you're going to—is in its own evolution. When you have a well-established, mature organization like Historic Annapolis, our response today would be different from what it would have been several decades ago when we were starting out.
>
> **Me:** What sort of difference are we talking about?
>
> **Greg:** Back then Mrs. Wright wouldn't share with anyone. She had one task and she stayed on it with great focus. She didn't want to have anything to do with any other organization in town. She wanted everyone to focus their energies entirely on Historic Annapolis and not on any other organization. And it worked.

Me: And now?

Greg: Today we want to share and expand the preservation world around us. We can and should assist groups like yours. But that takes time and resources away from other things.

Me: If that's the way you define your mission, what's the problem?

Greg: I don't know anyone sitting at a nonprofit organization thinking, "What can I do with my time? I don't have enough to do." So anytime you have an opportunity to work with others, you have to measure it very carefully against the fact that you'll be withdrawing resources from something else. It may be a *very* good idea to help get a historic district started elsewhere, because the two of us working together are going to strengthen preservation. But there is a cost to your own agenda.

Me: One of our concerns is that we won't see eye-to-eye and that'll weaken our community standing.

Greg: That's a real problem. When you're trying to build momentum you can't make room for all opinions and let people opt in and opt out. Mrs. Wright kept Historic Annapolis in crisis mode. If we don't do this *now* and *this way*, she'd say, then the community will have failed. She ended up with an effective organization that people loved or hated. No one was in the middle. You either approved of that kind of in-the-trenches, bare-knuckle, the-fight-must-be-won approach—*or* you said, "Oh, those Hysterical Annapolis people, they're just crazy." If you have to start with a take-no-prisoners attitude, you'll want everybody going in the same direction.

Me: Well, we're going all out to win. We assume there will be irreconcilable differences with some of our neighbors and other groups in the community.

Greg: And it's going to be hard for us to throw our hat into the arena that you must play in. Our priorities are different at this point. We're trying to work with all elements in the community rather than saying it's us against them.

Me: So what can you do for us?

Greg: We can counsel. We can pat you on the back and say "Atta' boy!" We have staff who can help you with preservation issues. One of the principal benefits of calling upon a mature organization is being able to point to it and say, "See, this is what we're trying to do, these people have done it, they think we're on the right track, they were at the same stage ten, fifteen, twenty years ago—and look at the good they've done. That's what we want to do." That helps you remove the issue from local personalities or a particular bone of contention. It's a role we certainly could play in community meetings or by testifying at critical hearings.

Me: How about personally? What can *Greg* do for us? I'll tell you straight out: We'd like you to join our steering committee and meet Tuesday evenings with us. What about it?

Greg: That's a serious issue, too. One would hope that a mature organization would be as generous as possible with its mentoring. It all comes down to a matter of resources and how much time we have.

Me: Sounds like you're saying, "No."

Greg: There are two problems here. The first is that everybody thinks they have to talk with the president and not with a staff person. Why? Because it just makes them feel better, even though staff may have just the hands-on experience they're looking for. It adds validity—if you have to report back to others you want to say, "I talked with the president." That's a fact of life for all organizations. People always want to talk with the person at the top.

Me: Sure. That's why I'm talking with you now.

Greg: But when it happens all the time, it puts a strain on the organization, especially if the higher up you go the more demands the organization itself is placing on its executive. It's a lot easier for me to delegate a staff member to go to another meeting, to spend two or three hours with you. But I couldn't do that myself all the time.

Me: We *are* trying to be respectful of your regular working schedule. That's why we're just talking about Tuesday *evenings* when you're off.

Greg: And that's the second issue: What's my commitment level? You've got a new group of all volunteers in your movement who are going to be passionate about your campaign. They're all charged up and won't think a thing about spending several hours at someone's home once a week. Sorry, that's not me.

Me: I appreciate your candor.

Greg: It's the difference between a new group and a well-established organization. Organizations have life cycles. At first volunteers do everything. The board is all volunteers. That's where you are. Then, if you succeed and stick with it, the organization begins to acquire staff. The board becomes more a board of directors. A mature organization has all the work done by a professional paid staff. The director becomes president and CEO with a board of trustees. And that's where we are.

Me: So it's not that we disagree on what's important; it's just that we see our work differently. Is that it?

Greg: Yes. It's one thing if you have passionate volunteers talking with passionate volunteers. But now you might be talking to someone who already works 40 or 50-plus hours a week as a paid employee. When you're all charged up it's easy to say, "*Of course*, that person will be *glad* to come out and help us because we're trying to do the same thing they did." In theory, that may be reasonable and true. But in reality, senior executives tend to have many commitments and might just not have the time or energy to give you. I also might have more academic or professional interests than a local activist who comes knocking on my door.

Me: *Time*, not *interest*, seems to be the constant issue here.

Greg: What you always hear people say who are in demand is that the most valuable thing for them is not money—it's time. And it really is true. As you get more senior what you really value more than anything is time to recharge your batteries by study and reflection. Sometimes you'd like to say, "I really can't come out to your meeting once a week on Tuesday evening because I'm just pooped." [Laughter.] But that's the way it is. You just can't say it.

Me: I've got an appointment to see you. What do you want to hear from me when I walk in the door?

Greg: Two things. *One*, I want to know *what* you really want. I don't want to hear you ask me, "What do I do?" I want you to come in and say, "Here's what we plan on doing and here's how we think you can fit into it." *Two*, I want you to tell me *why* you think I will fit in. Not, "You're head of Historic Annapolis and since we're doing something similar we know you'll want to be a part of it." I want to hear, "Here's what we'd like you to do: 1, 2, 3. And here's why. Will you do that?" Be specific. You can always be turned down. But at least you'll know why.

Me: Do you already know what you'd like me to ask you to do?

Greg: Yes. Ask me to explain our success story to your group. Ask for staff help to share their experiences in very specific areas. And when you get to the point where you need to go to the Mayor or the City Council and you want someone to go along who has been through the process successfully, I'll be glad to go along with you. I know these folks. I can help you make the contact. Those are the kinds of things we can do, and I think you'll be happy with them.

Me: What are sorts of specific things you *don't* want us to ask you to do?

Greg: I don't want to draw up documents, or be the one to arrange meetings. Don't ask us to conduct the survey of historic properties for the district. Things like that—things that others can do just as well.

Me: How about making a financial contribution toward the survey, if we're trying to do it ourselves?

Greg: That's interesting. That's something a more mature organization like ours might do. It would further preservation without drawing down our people resources.

Me: How about helping us find other sources of money?

Greg: That's a little trickier. The people we'd send you to are the same ones we go to. If they write a check for $100, I want it to come to us. Then we might be able to help you, maybe not.

Me: But you could help us find a consultant, put us in touch with a preservation law specialist, and identify other people at the state and local level we could use?

Greg: You bet. We should have the phone numbers on our Rolodex of all the people you're going to need. We should be willing to share that with you and tell you to tell them I said to give them a ring. Making those kinds of connections for you is easy to do, and it's the collegial thing to do. It also helps the people you call to know you're not coming in from left field.

Me: May we ask for help from your board members, or is that overstepping the line?

Greg: The board is one of our really valuable resources. My experience is that the bigger an organization gets, with maturity, the more prominent the board members become and the more willing they are to do that sort of thing. They don't have a lot of time but they can pick up the phone. They like to be considered decision shapers. If I were to call up and say, "We're working with a group, and we're going to see the Mayor, and it'd really help if you'd call and support them," they'd be delighted. They're happy to call their peers for you, because they're getting those kinds of calls all the time themselves. They like being able to say, "Now it's *your* turn."

Me: So in the final analysis, there are good reasons for coming to you—even if you're not going to be at the center of our effort.

Greg: Sure. You get our staff's help on my instructions. You get my help where I can give it. And you get the backing of our board. And I think that your readers should expect to get that kind of help from any organization like ours in their own locales.

Me: Thank you, Greg. That was enlightening.

Greg: It's been great to talk about these things. I hope it helps your readers.

We walked down the block to the City Dock. I looked around at the historic buildings fronting the water and at HAF's new history center. As Greg walked up a narrow side street to his office, I marveled at his organization's record of success upon success.

Then it struck me: There had been no HAF around to help out when HAF started! Experienced friends can help point the way, but we shape our victories ourselves.

TEN

A Practical Vision

In framing an ideal you may assume what you wish, but you must avoid impossibilities.

—Aristotle

Legendary CEO Jack Welch has said that good leaders are known by their ability to define an inspiring vision, to identify themselves with that vision, and to single-mindedly propel the vision forward to completion. The last part is the hard part. Without it, a vision is just pie in the sky.

ON PRESERVATION VALUES

Visit your local bookstore and look over the racks of leadership books. Many are full of advice on finding meaning, clarifying values, and putting them at the heart of your mission statement. These are *not* the kinds of books preservationists need. We've got that stuff down pat.

National, state, and, where available, local preservationists are eager to help you put together a values-packed vision for your community. All you have to do is ask, and maybe send off for a few pamphlets. Work hard at getting the districting details right and professional preservationists will buoy your confidence and fire your enthusiasm at every turn. I've been on the receiving end of such support, and it can be exhilarating . . . until you run up against someone like my friend "Noel," who has owned a Victorian inn. So here I am telling her about writing this book and she says, "Hel-*lo*! I care about old buildings, too, but why would anyone want to live in a historic district, you know, if they don't already have to?" Bummer. But instead of telling her to go pound salt, I realize, as Yogi Berra might say, you can hear a lot just by listening.

UP TO A POINT

First, her outburst puts us on notice. When we *think* preservation values and *say* historic district, she *hears* historic district and *thinks* government regulations. We don't have a *preservation* problem with her as much as we have a *districting* problem.

We need to stay alive to that difference. Just about everybody supports preservation values, but only *up to a point*. For you and me, districting is acceptable because it comes in under that point. For others, like Noel, it just doesn't. They may see districting as carrying too high a price in terms of other perceived goods, even if those goods are just conveniences.

If you listen closely—like Tracy Bailey of St. Cloud, Florida, does—you'll hear the same refrain time and again: "Many people support the historic district, but don't want more rules," she observes. Sonia Schmerl, ex-chair of Ann Arbor's HPC, is right to say that residents often are "more afraid of local government than they are of losing historic properties."

PRESERVATION-PLUS

Not all dissenters are dead set on breaking us. Advocacy may help some of them realize that protecting a legacy is important enough to bear districting. And the rest? How can we hook them?

Let me put it this way. When you go fishing, you don't use the bait you like; you use the bait the fish like—and you fish where the fish are, not where you want them to be.

Go to your neighbors. Find out what they value that historic districting can help them with. Start there. Is it security of property values? Commercial vitality? Residential quality of life? Ethnic or gender interests? Tourism? Infrastructure development? Roads, parking, and traffic control? Utilities? Environmental protection? Beautification? Schools? Adaptive reuse of closed churches or public buildings? What else?

Be attentive, be imaginative—and be aware that nobody just wants old buildings standing around. Preservation has to *lead* to somewhere better.

Think of it as "preservation-plus." A historic district can serve as a loom on which a whole tapestry of personal, corporate, and public interests may be interwoven. A district adds strength and identity to each individual thread—preservation included, but far from only preservation.

So whose interests can you pull together in your own community? The point is to be flexible, practical, broad, and welcoming.

Speak expansively of big-picture gains, yet give your vision a human scale. Make it relevant to each property owner. Pay them the respect they deserve by considering them as individuals. And always be honest with them.

Don't denigrate the power of selfish interests. The folks you're trying to attract have to be confident that the district won't unreasonably impede their ability to use their property as they wish. The more you attend to the interests of others, the less you have to do to win them to yours. But win them you must.

Offer them very tangible benefits as the quid pro quo for backing you. Inspire their eagerness for things that they cannot have as assuredly without historic districting, without your support and your leadership.

Never use preservation *against* anyone if you can help it. Leave no doubt that you're absolutely pro-growth, pro-business, pro-wealth, pro-prosperity, pro-tourism, pro-homeowners, pro-family values, *and pro-preservation through and through.*

Be the honey pot of possibilities, but don't forget the challenge at hand.

When we think politically, our primary objective isn't district designation. That's only what we want to get *out* of politics. But *in* the political process our main interest, right now, lies in gaining a competitive edge over our opponents.

So frame your vision to get that competitive edge. Foster the belief that designation is the event through which all other aspirations must pass, so that it becomes a practical instrument of their fulfillment too. Speak expectantly and often of districting as a watershed for the community. Lean into it. Politics exists, Aristotle said, for the sake of noble action. Think in terms of verbs, not nouns. Create a vision of achieving, not just achievement. Show them the contours of a journey that can capture their imagination and ignite enthusiasm. Call them to common purposes. Awaken them as civic beings sharing lives in a reimagined community that promises to give full play to their hopes and aspirations. Put your opponents on the wrong side of history.

Chief Justice of the Indiana Supreme Court—and preservationist—Randall Shepard has championed preservation for its focus on "community building." Historic districts, he argues, have become a form of community empowerment for influencing City Hall. They are the anvil on which new relationships, partnerships, and alliances are forged: perhaps, for example, with downtown commercial real estate interests, with various minority groups and their associations, and with leaders involved in public affairs.

This isn't just clever strategy. Most communities have a form of comprehensive planning. Our historic district has to make sense within the context of broader policies. City governments can be just as anxious as private citizens about being hobbled by regulations.

The surest way to deflate your opponents' mischaracterization of districting as imposing a repressive bureaucracy is to inspire others— private citizens and public officials alike—to recognize that what they really want aligns with preservation. Be a visionary to stretch their perspective, but be practical to seal their support.

THE POTTER AT THE WHEEL

Are you up to it? Of course you are. "Nothing convinces like conviction," Lyndon B. Johnson said. And beside the confidence of your beliefs, you know the political lay of the land in your community better than the professionals you need on the technical end of districting. This is *your* bailiwick.

A practical vision—one that appeals to people as you find them— can't be pulled out of thin air. It is part preservation practice and part sprung from your intimate knowledge of your friends and neighbors, of the unique combination of individual experiences and general characteristics that form the substance of your local situation.

You are like the potter at the wheel. Preservation values can shape a vision of what, ideally, you'd like to create. But your direct hands-on familiarity with the texture of community life gives you the feel of the practical craftsman for what you may reasonably expect to accomplish. Go ahead, roll up your sleeves. Plunge your hands into that pliable clay, work around your opponents, and bring forth from your community the best it has to give.

More prosaically, you will find your practical vision where your ambitions for preservation intersect political realities. It'll be made up of:

- What you want as framed by preservation principles.
- What your neighbors desire for themselves.
- What you should offer them concretely.
- What your neighbors will support.
- What you can accept.
- What you can get approved.

There's nothing formulaic here. Remember to think strategically. You are setting out to create the political context for your success. Support and opposition will grow or shrink as your own campaign evolves. It'll seem that every time you drive a stake in the ground, the ground shifts on you.

Keep in mind that good folks can back a historic district for any number of reasons on which there does not have to be common agreement. Preservation may be *your* reason, but don't ask others to take a loyalty oath to it.

ON PRINCIPLE AND PRAGMATISM

This message—not to let pursuit of the ideal get in the way of what's attainable—can be perplexing, especially for idealists, and we preservationists are a pretty idealistic lot. How about you?

If we're going to be any good at preservation politics, we're going to have to learn to think in two different ways simultaneously when confronted with a policy choice:

- As idealists, as people who embrace general standards of right, we will always ask how our decision accords with preservation principles.
- But as political activists, committed to advancing the standing of preservation in our community, we must also question how a decision affects our chances of winning.

Unfortunately, the answer to one often doesn't square easily with the other.

At a very human level, it's extremely hard for us to accept that the only way we can advance what we care about is by acting in ways that are likely to end up compromising it. But I don't want you to feel unfairly put upon as a preservationist. There's nothing peculiar to you in this dilemma. It's been around all of politics at least since the early Greeks first started sweating over it.

Can you handle it? Let me give you a very simple example out of my own experience in starting a rural historic district in Oak Ridge, North Carolina.

Suppose I told you that we announced during our campaign that vinyl-coated aluminum siding would not be prohibited by our design guidelines? Would your first response be a principled, "Oh, no!"? Or would it be a more politically perceptive "Why?"

I'll tell you why. We did it because of political calculations. First, we had bigger fish to fry. Unless we got the historic district, a superhighway would bisect the village and bring far greater pressures to bear on historic resources, property values, and local institutions like our antebellum military prep academy. Then, too, our County Commission was not at all well disposed toward our effort. Caught between its preference for 100 percent property owner support or exempting many acres of buildable open farmland at the highway intersection, we chose to force the issue with overwhelming community support. So our second concern was to keep our numbers in the upper ranges.

Aluminum siding was popular in Oak Ridge. Even more so was the young family man in our midst whose livelihood depended on it, as a critical few neighbors pointed out. We did what we figured we had to do. The issue was simply too important to be left to preservation.

So what will you do if a similar situation arises? Unfortunately for some of our friends, ideology seizes them like rigor mortis, incapacitating intelligent movement, making them dead to their real interests. No matter how righteous you think it is, you can't let your vision of a well-preserved community select all your political options for you.

ON COURAGE AND CONVICTION

Everywhere we turn today it seems some politician is taking pride in standing on principle against an alleged tide of compromise. But you and I know, unless we're gullible, that politics isn't just about principle. If it were, all we'd have to do is declare the principle that settles the policy and then go home. No, politics is about the far more interesting problem of what you do with principle when real life demurs.

Having the courage of your convictions doesn't mean acting in divine disregard of present realities. Lead from conviction, by all means, but be pragmatic about the big picture. What works is the right political choice. What's more, it's the right moral choice too, because winning is the only way you can move forward any part of your preservation agenda for the benefit of your community.

I think Kevin Ebberle, the preservation-minded president of Charleston's Hampton Park Terrace Neighborhood Association, appreciates the point. In a city where the Board of Architectural Review (BAR) holds sway on the historic peninsula, he talks of a "BAR-lite" oversight regime for his proposed district bordering on The Citadel.[1] To insist on more would be self-defeating.

Conviction instills you with courage. And it is courage you need for doing those things, here and now, that you'd rather avoid.

To this day I don't really know if we had to exempt aluminum siding in Oak Ridge. I do know our ranks held. Minutes before the final vote, a key commissioner asked if on behalf of our group I would agree to exclude the acreage at the intersection in order to assure passage. With a high degree of popular support behind me, but unable to consult with the neighbors whose trust I held, I rolled the dice.

As it turned out, a one-vote majority of the county commissioners approved our district after a two-year campaign. The highway plan bypassed us. A decade later, the academy prospers and aluminum siding is still an option on noncontributing structures. It's less than we might have hoped for, but more than we came close to having.

In my opinion, the so-called leader who listens only to the single steady voice of principle is just as inconsiderate of the public interest as one who heeds no principles at all. The former rarely wins. The latter is seldom right.

When you win, what you manage to achieve will always be judged in terms of preservation values. And believe me, someone who has stood on the sidelines will find you wanting.

But take heart. No one stands for principle on firmer ground than the conscientious activist who finds a practical way to win.

NOTE

1. Bill Davis, "Hampton Park Smackdown," Charleston, SC, *City Paper*, January 12, 2005.

ELEVEN

Thinking Politically about Design Guidelines

Many people have accused me of being devious. They may be right.

—Archy McNally in Lawrence Sanders,
McNally's Puzzle

Sooner or later you, too, will have to talk with your neighbors about how strictly the historic district will oversee what they do to their properties. When the time comes, you'll want to practice a little creative ambiguity.

Does that sound devious to you? Try to see it my way. A studied—yet honest—vagueness is an essential political skill.

The problem couldn't be plainer. We have to sell our neighbors on our vision of what the historic district can do for them. That means that our proposal has to be strict enough to preserve the legacy that is the key to everything else. But the more restrictive we make it, the more likely it is to encounter opposition.

Our political task, then, is to warm our neighbors to the historic district's benefits without overheating their anxieties about its costs. That isn't just a political necessity. It's also being responsible to them.

The truth is that most property owners will rarely engage the district's review procedures after designation. And when they do, only a few will occasionally feel a regulatory pinch. If we don't discourage wild imagining now about how bad it could be, then we run the risk of losing the district—and that would be unforgivable.

So if you're to be a successful leader, you're going to have to help folks choose what is good in spite of themselves. If that's being devious, then let's be all for it.

YOUR CHOICE

The basic issue facing us here is whether—or how and to what extent—we'll make design guidelines part of our districting campaign.

If you live in Wilmington, North Carolina, or a town like it, you have no choice. Kaye and Maggie told us in chapter 4 that our new district would be brought in under an already existing ordinance and a full set of guidelines, with maybe a tweak or two. The advantage there is that folks can see how the district has actually worked on behalf of property owners in practice.

Elsewhere, you may be obliged by statute or instruction to submit your guidelines along with the designation proposal. In most locales, however, guidelines just have to be adopted before the HPC starts issuing certificates of approval.

There is, you understand, no such thing as a generic historic district. Property owners are bound to ask specific questions about specific work activities. They'll want to know:

- Which work activities will require full HPC design review and approval.

- Which activities may require simple on-the-spot staff approval.
- Which ones may be done without any oversight at all.

Still, other issues impinge. Will the HPC, for example, be given say-so over changes not visible from the street? Will noncontributing properties be treated differently? Questions like these may be anticipated in the district ordinance itself, but one way or another they'll influence public interest in knowing more about design guidelines.

So the question remains: How much are you going to say and how will you say it? In the end, your ability to win over supporters depends on whether they trust you.

TO DRAFT OR NOT TO DRAFT?

So what do we have to do to earn their trust? Should we be drafting guidelines to show them? My answer is a firm "perhaps, perhaps not." You're simply going to have to decide what to do without any certainty that it's the right choice.

Informed opinion is divided. Some think it helps a campaign to have guidelines in hand. Others see it as an ill-advised complication.

What are folks—professional preservationists and city planners, your friends and allies—telling you? Keep in mind that making them at ease with your decision is a part of your political challenge, too.

So let's parse the problem. If we—let's say you and I, our steering committee, and a professional consultant or staffer—write up guidelines now that we'll propose to the HPC later, breakers will say we're being dictatorial. But if we're seen as refusing to submit what we have in mind to public scrutiny, they'll portray us as trying to sell the community a pig in a poke before designation.

On the other hand, if we open up the process now to all interested parties—friends and foes and undecideds all—then the guidelines will become yet another costly battleground in the districting fight. Even if we win the battle and the war, the guidelines will bear the marks of those who opposed them in the first place.

A MIDDLE COURSE GAMBIT

The best way to be trusted is to be candid with your neighbors. Tell them that the main question before us right now is simply whether we want the benefits of having a historic district. Once we decide that—once everyone's onboard who's coming aboard—then we'll get together and decide on agreeable guidelines. But ask them to hold off until then.

But why would they agree to that? Well, put yourself in their place. You see what districting can do for you and you're beginning to see that it's worth a price—that, as my friend Frank Whitaker has said, "The juice is worth the squeeze." Now then, that being the case, wouldn't you want to make sure that the hands that'll do the squeezing are friendly?

So when you talk with them, commit to making the drafting process open—*but not just yet*. They should see that if we were to open it up now, breakers would do their best to make every aspect of the guidelines as onerous as possible to defeat us. It'd be plain dumb to let them in on what the rest of us will have to live with after designation.

Those who are considering their options have to know they can't just stand aside, either, waiting to see what happens. Sure, when the time comes everyone will have a chance to voice their opinions. But leave no doubt in their minds—though do it diplomatically—*that what they do today with us to win the district will decide how their voices will be heard tomorrow.*

There's nothing devious in this. We're offering takers some bankable benefits for making the right choice.

TWELVE

It's Personal

All this criticism—it's like ducks off my back.

—Samuel Goldwyn

Where all politics is local, all preservation is personal. Every historic district is a slamdunk great idea for fifteen minutes. That's about as long as it takes for people to start taking it to heart.

"I'm surprised by the intensity of the opposition," Mary McWilliams says in Evanston, Illinois.[1] Really? If *you* can get excited about property you don't own, you have to expect passion from those who do.

Historic districts hit home, literally. They touch us where we live and often how we earn our living.

But it's never just about the money. Anyone who says, "It's only business, nothing personal," is nuts. Folks may talk money, but it's like their own pictures were on every dollar bill. Touch one and you've laid hands on them and their families.

CHAPTER TWELVE

No, districting economics, like its politics, is intensely personal, too.

THE ATTACK

You're the messenger. Expect personal attacks.

Acquaintances may stop speaking to you. But it beats hearing them say—as others have in other places—that you're "arrogant," "sniveling," "frightening," "false," "obnoxious," "effete," and even—this from Seattle—fired by "yuppie-paradise, coffee fiend pretensions."

They're mad, for sure. But what we want to know is whether they're politically smart, too. To get a handle on that, we have to look past what they say to see how they're shaking your tree.

It's all too easy to be rattled by the variety of opponents you can encounter, from the serious to the frivolous, rational to emotional, honest to dishonest, vocal and active to silent and passive, in-your-face hostile to behind-your-back-sneaky. You may, of course, run after every one of these detractors, trying to set the record straight. Play their game and you'll wear yourself out.

Dealing with the opposition is like courting the memory challenged girl in the movie *50 First Dates*. Each time there's a meeting you have to start all over again with the same people. It's like they remember nothing! They raise the same old questions, level the same charges, tell the same lies, commit the same slanders . . . and pile on more of the same. Nothing we say will change them. As it is, we're the ones who have to adjust our expectations.

THE TACTIC

Don't think that your adversaries will ask you questions to have them answered, or raise issues to have them resolved, or make factual errors to have them corrected. Forget about it.

They're only interested in subverting your case for districting. If they can do it through misdirection and disinformation, so much the better. They want to frustrate you, anger you, make you lash out, lead you into paths of condescension. They'll challenge your skills more than your intellect, and do all in their power to make you look the fool, the hack, the petty tyrant. The last thing they want is for others to take you seriously.

And you know what? No one has to take them seriously, either, for them to beat the socks off of you:

- They don't have to make a case, just prevent you from making yours.
- They don't have to have a vision of their own, just sow doubt about the one you're pushing.
- They don't have to do anything, just prevent anything else from being done.

So you go to meetings stoked to advocate preservation and they give you Greta Garbo: "The major thing we want is to be left alone," says a New England dairy farmer says who has land for development.

Ironic, isn't it? We have to change the law to preserve the community. But if they can keep the law as it is, then they can pretty much change whatever they like.

DEFENSE OF THE FAMILIAR

Unfortunately for us, there are a lot of takers out there in the middle ground of public opinion who'd be happy if the issue just disappeared. Whether he means to or not (and I can't decide which), ninety-three-year-old Dearborn resident Ed Klein gives comfort to our opponents when he simply says, "I'd like to see things stay the way they are."[2]

It's a common refrain. To our ears it harbors inconsistency. What "things" does he have in mind? He can't possibly mean both the zoning law *and* the community, can he? Well, I think yes, he does.

Don't go looking for logic in politics. Many people don't parse these problems in terms of ends and means. Even if they do, they may ignore the conclusions. When it comes to where they live, they just don't want to lose the familiar.

You can talk till you're blue in the face that disorienting change is coming. And they look at you as if to say, "Yeah, tell me about it." You see yourself as a preservationist, the one who assures them of continuity. They see you as the present face of change, what with your new historic district and all. "And," they think to themselves, "*you're* asking *us* for *our* help to keep things as they *are*?!"

That other change you've been warning them about—the loss of this or that distinctive characteristic of the community—is, for a lot of good folks, just too abstract, too "iffy," too distant a prospect to get worked up over right now. Even if some current project is kicking up a ruckus, that kind of change is familiar. "Happens all the time," they'll say.

But the district? That's a different story. They know if it happens they can't duck it, and that scares a good many of them.

We wouldn't have to work nearly so hard at advocacy if the philosophy, law, institutions, and procedures of historic preservation weren't so unfamiliar and unsettling to the average property owner. People just don't want to wait to hear you out before they get all cranked up over it, either.

EXCOMMUNICATION

They start with the silly snicker about "hysterical" preservation. Then third-hand horror stories from other historic districts get passed around. Next, half-baked ideas are swapped over backyard fences and in the checkout line. Opinions are quickly formed on the thinnest of pretexts. Disagreements follow.

Soon someone's accusing you of —do you see it coming?— "dividing the neighborhood." This is a pronouncement of excommunication in a community, so be prepared to deal with it.

Keep your composure. Politics happens. It's nobody's particular fault. Folks have interests and interests collide. That's all.

Blame is just a tactic, not a reality. Don't fall for their ploy.

It takes two to tango. The more you protest your innocence or make excuses, the more it'll smell like guilt on a sinner. Think about what the character Max said in the film *8MM*. "When you dance with the Devil, the Devil don't change. The Devil changes you."

A GRACIOUS DISPENSATION

Stick to the moral high ground. But be not self-righteous.

We all struggle *privately* with the conflict between what we desire for ourselves and what's good for the community. Districting brings that conflict out into the open. We get up in front of our neighbors and ask them to commit one way or the other, to stand with us for community or go their separate ways.

This call to a *public* decision is finally what makes districting so intensely personal. It publicly asks each of us as private individuals and citizens to make difficult choices that will affect the way we are viewed by others.

Carol W. DeGrasse of the Property Rights Foundation of America seems to admit as much. "This controversy," she wrote of the proposed, minimally restrictive Glimmerglass National Register District around Cooperstown, New York, "unfairly pits individuals who are concerned about regulation of their homes and businesses against people who would like to protect the historical beauty of the area."[3]

"Unfairly"? This is a personal complaint, not a policy difference. It's as if it were rude, uncalled for, or—in the words of one
Santa Monican—"not proper" to hold each other accountable for
how we choose between freedom and responsibility.

They say we're dividing the community. But it's this internal division between self and community that is at the root of their anger.
You see what the real problem is, don't you? We're dealing with
conflicted souls here. So the grace with which you handle the most
obnoxious adversary will say more about your leadership than your
most clearly reasoned argument or witty riposte.

NOTES

1. Jane Adler, "Preservation Haul," www.chicagotribune.com,
Chicago Tribune Online Edition, December 28, 2003.

2. Craig Garrett, "Historic Designation Pits Neighbors in Dearborn,"
www.detnews.com, *The Detroit News*, September 7, 2001.

3. Carol W. DeGrasse, "Questions Historic District," www.prfamerica
.org, letter to the editor published in *Freeman's Journal*, Cooperstown,
NY, May 7, 1999.

THIRTEEN

Sticks and Stones

Silence is the unbearable repartee.

—G. K. Chesterton

Some people are born ugly, but others are self-made men. Here's a list of words they've used against us, taken from many actual designation fights. Tape them to your mirror and read them aloud. Get used to their sound because you're going to hear some of them in public. Learn to smile back. A friend of mine says that people never disappoint him; they always live down to his expectations. Just don't let them shake your soda.

hysterical
nosy
fanatical
arrogant
false
busybody
extremist
elitist
sinister
sniveling
obnoxious
self-appointed
priggish
obscurantist
paranoid
overreaching
frightening
outsider
mean
censorious
pseudo-intellectual
dishonest
history buff
overeducated
Volvo volunteer
petty fetishist
whimsical
dictatorial
whining
careless
uncaring
idolatrous
arbitrary
controlling
zealous
romanticist
strange
dreary
sad
cavalier
comical

YOUR PICTURE HERE

laughable
sick
nasty
sorry
out-of-touch
statist
self-important
power hungry
grasping
insane
un-American
tyrannical
strident
pious
reactionary
liberal
fascist
left-wing
inquisitor
blood-sucking
cultist
brainwashed
ill-mannered
unhappy
desperate
frustrated
scared
pitiful

stupid
silly
ludicrous
fruitcake
slick
fuzzy minded
liar
yuppie
rat
rat bastard
troglodyte
jerk
new comer
old timer
senile
unpatriotic
enemy
idiotic
dreamer
house hugger
preachy
haughty
foolish
spoiler
storm trooper
Gestapo
spy
informer
underhanded
harebrained
crazy
gullible
masochistic
sadistic
highfalutin
grandee
over-educated
naive
snake-in-the-grass
spend thrift

Figure 13.1

FOURTEEN

The Campaign Kickoff

Gentlemen, it is better to have died as a small boy than to fumble this football.

—John Heisman

Every districting campaign should begin with a public kickoff. This is when you announce your intentions and state your case.

But bear in mind what also happens during a kickoff. Just like in football, we put the ball in our opponents' hands and try to keep them from running it back on us.

Influence is the yardage of politics. We're always in the process of gaining, holding, or losing it. It's not enough that we know our goal. Our opening play has to be designed to pin our opponents deep in their own territory and hold them there.

I want you to get ready now for that initial grassroots meeting in the district. It's your best chance to establish excellent position.

THE COMMUNITY MEETING

Unofficial community meetings—and you should have two or more—are an opportunity and a challenge:

1. Early meetings can help head off charges that the district is a done deal with the City or that we're complicit in making an end run around the community.
2. They help us squelch rumors and correct misinformation.
3. They provide us opportunities to persuade others through advocacy.
4. They may settle at least some neighborhood differences over districting before we appear in front of official decision makers.
5. They offer us an opportunity to gauge and isolate our opposition as we head into the formal designation process.
6. They give us a chance to hone our message.
7. They provide a forum for building public confidence in our leadership.

They are also the best setting for talking to our neighbors about *community itself* before heading downtown to the polarizing public hearings that always seem to be filled with talk of "what I think," "what I want," and "what I need."

Of course if we fumble our chances, these meetings can put us in an even more unfavorable light, harden differences, and give our opponents a chance to make significant gains at our expense.

FALSE STARTS

The hardest part of a districting campaign for political novices may be knowing how to step out of the crowd and lead. It isn't easy even with experience. So I want you to imagine yourself getting up in front of your neighbors. Look them in the eye now and tell me what you see.

No, on second thought let me tell you. What you see are people who deserve your best effort. Don't worry about what they think of you personally for doing this. The main thing is they're here to listen to what you have to say.

Once you've crossed the floor to the front of the room, you've set yourself apart as a *leader*. Don't fall into the trap of acting like a *facilitator*:

- Don't start out by deferring to your neighbors.
- Don't act like the initiative has to come from them.
- Don't ask them how they *feel* about historic districts.
- Don't ask them what they want to do.
- Don't ask them how they want to proceed.

This may be a *community* meeting but it's not *their* meeting. They didn't call it. You did. It's *your* meeting. You're here for one reason only, and that is to sell them on your practical vision and get them to back the district.

Anything that keeps you from getting directly to your message is a false start from which it is tough to recover. Let me give you a few examples.

1. The Open-Ended Forum

I hear it again and again in tales of woe. It's like in the country song, how can anything that feels so right be so wrong?

You're excited by the idea of a historic district, so you get a few people together and call a community meeting to let everyone in on it. Once the basic facts are in evidence, you toss out the fatal open-ended question to the crowd—"Well, what do you think?"

This seems to be the right thing to do—to be seen bringing a good idea to your neighbors while showing yourself to be a good listener, not above others, and trusting of their judgment. Yet it is so wrong. It puts feelings—including how people feel about you—above policy. It's form at the expense of substance.

Don't ask people what they think until you've really given them something to think about. Otherwise you're just inviting trouble—a litany of criticism, dissent, silly comments, "what-ifs," and people talking about all sorts of other community issues.

2. The Public Study Committee

A variation on the theme is having a blue-ribbon committee conduct a public feasibility study that ends with a recommendation. It's supposed to be objective, of course. But anything that's intended to lead to legislation is always thoroughly political. Think about how a committee might be formed:

- Who will decide who's on the committee?
- Will they try to make it "fair and balanced" rather than focused and purposeful?
- Will preservationists be said to be too biased to be included?
- Will you be considered too political to be put on it?
- Who will draft the report, and who will present it?
- Who will define what "feasible" means?

And if the district's *political* feasibility is made part of the study, then what?

A study committee might well decide to conduct its own opinion survey *prior* to reporting out a developed district plan. If they (or we) go about polling neighbors on how they feel about districting before we take to the field, we'll have them deciding the game before seeing it played. And don't you think our opponents know that the best time to stop us is before we get started?

And if you can't avoid a separate study committee? In Massachusetts, for instance, the state Historical Commission specifies that, in the absence of an established HPC, a locally designated committee appointed by the City Council will conduct a property owner opinion survey, prepare educational materials, hold informational meetings, and prepare a preliminary study report. If that's your lot, then say everything nice, and find an accommodation. But don't relinquish the political initiative.

3. The Open Huddle

It's not a good idea, either, to advertise an early get-together for "anyone interested in a historic district." You can't have a meeting with some neighbors without causing problems with others in the long run.

What's to be gained anyway? You know the folks you're inviting will expect some kind of presentation from you, and anything you say will soon be common knowledge. If you're ready to talk to a few, then why not talk to everybody at once? There's a lot to be said for openness once we get to the kickoff. But if we let opponents into our huddle, we have to like their chances.

4. The Offside Call

Suppose we don't make any false starts. Say we get it right. We set the agenda, run the meeting, state our case . . . and soon someone's blowing a whistle on us. Our infraction? We jumped offside. We didn't ask them first. We get penalized for being arrogant, elitist, even conspiratorial.

So it's damned if we do, damned if we don't, isn't it? We go to the community either too soon or we go too late. Either way, we're going to lose ground.

The best we can do is hold our first community meeting as quickly as possible. We can't wait to get it perfect. At some point we'll just have to stop the attrition by suspicion and take to the field.

And finally this, if a sense of urgency hasn't seeped in yet: there's always a danger that our opponents will jump the gun and call their own "stop the historic district" meeting first.

FIFTEEN

Community Meeting Arrangements

Before everything else, getting ready is the secret of success.

—Henry Ford

A community meeting is no casual pickup game among friends. Historic districting is big-league politics to those involved no matter how small the community. Expect to be hit at every turn.

Of course, you might not end up bruised and battered. You know your own situation and might expect an easy go of it. But don't underestimate the value of being prepared for the worst.

Some folks will take exception to what you *say*. But has it occurred to you that meeting arrangements have political implications, too? Critics will jump on even minor errors to discredit the process.

THE MEETING PLACE

If your meeting venue is owned or managed by supporters, then opponents may say they felt unwelcome or intimidated. It's simply astounding how large the mere *appearance* of fairness looms in local politics.

Select a convenient neutral site if you can, such as a public school or community center. If you use a public facility, make sure you pay for it and get a receipt. If there is no charge, get it in writing. Watch the date and time, too. For instance, avoid a football Saturday afternoon if you're in a university community.

MAILINGS

Notify *all* property owners by mail. Be a little paranoid. The first law of mailings is to assume that any announcement that can go astray will go astray if it's addressed to an eventual opponent. Double check your address labels against the list you developed earlier (chapter 7). Use certified mail if you've got the budget for it.

Don't wait till the last minute. Hell hath no fury like a retiree wintering in Arizona who gets his forwarded mail after a meeting's come and gone. A notice that arrives late is the same as one not sent at all.

Remember: it's illegal to put unstamped circulars in mailboxes or through mail slots. Your opponents will have a field day with that fumble.

Why the concern? When the going gets ugly, the ugly complain about fairness and due process—even though due process doesn't apply to informal community meetings. An alleged failure to notify is just the kind of infraction that politicians find hard to ignore.

Sample Announcement

Interest has been expressed in designating our neighborhood a local historic district. You are cordially invited to a community meeting at **(location)** on **(date & time)**.

If you cannot attend, please visit our website at **www.(name) .org** or contact **(name, address, e-mail, and telephone)** to have materials and announcements of future meetings sent to you.

THE ANNOUNCEMENT

Say as little as possible in the meeting announcement so it will get read. Use the passive voice to keep focus on the meeting, not you.

Use a large font for folks with impaired vision. Put key information in boldface type. Sign it from your steering committee. Make sure the return address lies inside the proposed district.

Andy Rooney has said on *60 Minutes* that he routinely throws away any mail that begins with, "Dear Property Owner." You've got a computer. Use it. Personalize every letter.

INVITING OTHER PARTICIPANTS

Assure that the **City Planning Department** is represented. Settle in advance what you expect of them. They're there to lend authority to what you say and to help with procedural questions. Some staff prefer to avoid confrontational meetings and others may take an unhelpful officious attitude toward the public. It's better to go it alone than go that route with them.

Your own **preservation specialist**—if you've managed to enlist one—should handle technical questions. Extend an invitation to your **State Historic Preservation Office** to help quell doubts about your objectivity while supporting you on matters of state law.

Be sure to invite private-sector opinion **shapers** who support districting. Talk with them first, however. Make sure that they understand your agenda and how you'll conduct the meeting. Work out what they can contribute and how you'll use them.

Look at any **other constituencies** besides property owners that you think will benefit from districting. If one of your goals is revitalizing retail business, then invite business owners. If it's keeping the old elementary school open, then invite the PTA. Invite any other groups whose absence would be a political faux pas.

How about the local **press**? It's never too early to start working the media. But as we'll see in chapter 27, reporters seek out controversy—because editors like it—and they will inflate your opponents' claims just for the sake of "balanced" reporting. It's better to invite a specific reporter you can prep ahead of time than to have to deal with one who just shows up cold.

Make a list of the most important people you want to see at the meeting. Have your steering committee call each one to remind them as the meeting approaches.

ROOM SETUP AND GREETING

Think carefully about seating. I'd advise you to ignore meeting consultants who want to diminish conflict by breaking into small groups around tables, each with its own moderator. We don't want to give our critics cause to say they were sidelined.

Do whatever helps you perform well. But I think that if you're going to lead, then you ought to get on your feet—never sit down—and lead from the front. Your opponents are sure to claim later that this made it *your* meeting, not a *community* meeting. But once you give up center stage you'll never get it back.

As folks arrive, greet them with a member of your committee, a sign-in sheet, the petition, name tags, and 3x5 cards and pencils for follow-up questions and comments—and e-mail addresses. Give everyone a copy of your "Frequently Asked Questions" (FAQs) that we'll cover in chapter 17. Make sure printed material has your website on it, and post the site prominently at the front of the room.

Welcome everyone as warmly as possible—or at least cordially. If anybody jumps to an attack, just smile and ask them to keep an open mind. Don't let your colleagues stand around in cliques. They should be working the room, conveying friendliness, enthusiasm, and confidence.

And for heaven's sake, make sure the room is set up properly before anyone arrives. Nothing erodes public confidence like hearing you blame others for facility problems—a dead microphone, not enough chairs, a locked restroom. If you can't take care of getting the room right, how can you be entrusted with a district?

THE MAP TRAP

Hang a survey map of the proposed district at the front of the room, with the survey consultant standing by to answer questions. You'll soon understand that geography is political destiny.

How the map is derived can be political dynamite. It has to be defensible in preservation terms, with a density of contributing historic properties sufficient to justify districting. But no one benefits if the district is *technically* defensible yet *politically* unwinnable. Where the density of contributing properties thins out on the district's periphery, the question of including or excluding a street or block is a close call.

If the boundaries are still not firmed up by meeting time, make this abundantly clear by posting "DRAFT" across the map's top. No matter what you say, the opposition will probably complain later that the whole designation process was untrustworthy because "the map kept changing on us."

Make sure the map covers the maximum probable territory. You might get away with reducing the district later, but not expanding it. When the map is finally set, say so, and then leave it alone no matter what. That's the best you can do.

CIRCULATING YOUR PETITION

On your "top ten" list of things to get done at the meeting #1 is maximizing the number of folks you get to sign your petition (see chapter 23). I'll be cold-blooded about this. Nothing you do to educate for preservation is worth much if it doesn't put signatures on your petition. Anybody can be for *preservation*. But only a signature registers support for *districting*. Politics has a built-in bias favoring numbers. And the only numbers that politicians will believe are those you have documented and verified.

Any name *not* on your petition will be presumed to be a property owner against you. Opponents always get the benefit of the doubt.

Work out a plan for canvassing the meeting. Make it easy for people to sign, but don't expect them to wait in line. Circulate clipboard copies before and after the meeting. Keep friendly hands on them. Tell your petition managers to steer clear of one-on-one arguments. If they get tied up in a knot of folks listening to attacks, then your opponents win.

Make sure your managers are eager and unapologetic about asking for support. Their attitude should be that signing is an opportunity not a favor.

Never, ever, let yourself get so caught up in the ebb and flow of the meeting that you lose sight of your goal. Nothing is more self-defeating than ending the meeting and then shouting out, "Oh yes—don't forget to sign the petition on your way out!" *No point that you'll make in the meeting will be as important tomorrow as the points you score on the petition today.*

Everybody exiting should have to pass by someone asking them to sign before they get out the door. Don't miss that chance. Be sure those who refuse are remembered.

COMMENT CARDS

I've suggested comment cards because you want to know what people are thinking. They also give folks a chance to blow off steam and then think better of it before expressing anger in public.

If you can print cards, include a place for name and address, plus a check-box for requesting a personal follow-up at a specified phone number or e-mail address. Be sure to collect comment cards at the end of the meeting and follow through on requests for information without delay.

RECORD THE PROCEEDINGS

Video, audio, or scribe. One way or another keep a record of what transpires. When you get to the Q&A, keep a record of what each questioner says. This is the raw data you'll need for refuting any later claim that opponents were shut out from participating in your meetings.

Keep the ball rolling by announcing the next community meeting before adjourning.

THE DAY AFTER

Get together with your steering committee ASAP to discuss how things went and to agree on what to do next. Move quickly, preferably within a day or two, to contact folks who registered serious questions or who looked like they could be persuaded your way.

Whatever you do, don't leave the Monday morning quarterbacking to your opponents. Be seen out and about talking up the historic district.

SIXTEEN

Your Community Presentation

I only speak right on; I tell you that which you yourselves
do know. . . .

—William Shakespeare, *Julius Caesar*

"I am no orator," Mark Antony next told the crowd at Caesar's fu-
neral. And you? Do you, too, say you "have neither wit, nor words
. . . nor the power of speech, to stir men's blood"?

Don't sell yourself short. Like Antony you have conviction
and a compelling subject. Like him, you know the time, the setting, the audience, and what motivates them to listen. The words
will come.

But how little time there is to get your message across! Think.
How long would *you* sit still for you? Let's be optimistic. You'll
have some twenty minutes to introduce districting and to make
your case. After that, it's all questions and answers.

We're going to make the Q&A session work for you. Handled right, it'll free you from numbing details in your opening presentation. Shakespeare gave Antony thirty-five lines to capture the crowd's attention, and then multiples of that in dialog with citizens to bend them to his purpose. So let's see what *we* can do for you.

THINKING AND WRITING

Twenty minutes to fill with words—a very few words, to be on the safe side. What will you say? Be brief, but beware: brief is hard. Charles Dickens once was asked why he wrote such long novels. "Madam," he replied, "I haven't the time to make them short." Let's take time now to get ours right.

Start with your practical vision for the community. Put it into words and write them down. Don't worry about brevity yet. Read what you've written out loud. How does it sound to your own ear? Does it say what you want it to say? Be honest with yourself. If it doesn't sound right, it probably isn't right.

Don't tell me that you're having problems with writing. There are no writing problems. There are only thinking problems. If you know what you think, you can write it down. Writing is the best self-test of clear thinking. The clearer your thinking, the clearer your writing will be and the better it'll sound to you. And the clearer your thinking, the fewer the words you'll need to express your thoughts.

Just make sure you don't muddy it up with jargon. Preservationists can have difficulty with plain English. Don't speak of "historic fabric" when you mean old siding, windows, doors, and roofing materials. Normal folks will think you're talking about draperies.

Jargon is tempting shorthand. But I think the poet Horace gave us fair warning: "It is when I struggle to be brief that I become obscure."

SPEAKING AS THINKING FOR OTHERS

Thinking. Writing. Now speaking. You may think and write what sounds good to you. Political speech is for other ears.

Sometimes it just means telling folks what they want to hear. But if you want to *lead* them, then speak so that they recognize your expressed words as their own inarticulate thoughts made clear.

Leadership involves doing other people's thinking for them, winnowing out contradictory values and impulses, and getting them to act on the conclusions we promote. That's why our main targets are those takers in the middle whose minds aren't made up yet.

What you'll say is framework for the longer dialog they'll be having with themselves once you get their attention. So give them the outline that takes them where you want them to go.

YOUR APPROACH

Surprise your listeners. They're expecting a history lesson and talk about regulations. Some are ready to pounce. Others just don't see what preservation has to do with them. So take a different tack.

Start with them and their interests. Talk about what *they* know first. This will get you beyond the blandishments—such as protecting our unique architectural history—and connect your purposes to their concerns—like property values. Then you can begin leading them into new ways of thinking about their investments in the community.

It's like the way preservation itself works to fit new construction into an older community. You can successfully introduce a new idea to your listeners as long as it's compatible with the existing architecture of their thought. This is how, as Samuel Johnson said of poets, "New things are made familiar, and familiar things made new." Make the familiar work for you.

Don't be the first one to raise objections to districting just because you believe you ought to address what *you think* will trouble your neighbors. There'll be time enough for that in the Q&A period.

Don't explain *yourself*, either. Explain the *district*. State your case as fact, not argument. Make it a seamlessly positive presentation, and always talk up—never down—to your audience. That will underscore your confidence that they are up to this task.

The Outline

What follows is intended only to show you what I mean. Use it to jump-start your thinking. Reshape it to your own liking and your own community's situation. Polish it till you can hit each point with a very few sentences.

- Introductions and explanation that this is an informal community meeting, not an officially mandated due process public hearing.
- Begin with your listeners' **invested interests in property**.
- Remind them what **they care about in the community** that supports those interests: e.g., quality of life, security, family, and business values.
- Link this to **preservation values**: e.g., identity of place, stewardship of community resources, rooted growth.
- Establish the **preservation case** for districting, including the map's rationale.
- Make vivid the **situation** around them that has led you to bring this proposal forward—but make a villain of no one. If there is a crisis, this is the time to nail it down.
- Stress that you take no pleasure in putting difficult choices before the community, but that now is the **time for all of us to step up.** "Where is the man," Rousseau asked, "who owes nothing to the land in which he lives?"
- Create a sense of a community ready to embrace **change as opportunity**. Make it clear that a zoning overlay district doesn't stop change, but it can facilitate and shape growth.
- Stress good-naturedly that **2,000 historic districts** must be on to something.

- Make them alive to the **possibilities** awaiting them. As benefits are for all, responsibilities must be borne by all.
- Build **anticipation** through concrete examples taken from the experiences of similar communities.
- Drive home the idea that districting is **empowerment** (versus an oppressive layer of government), giving individuals and the community a greater say in City Hall over decisions that affect them.
- Stress that we, not the government, are doing this **ourselves**.
- Give a brief **synopsis of how the district will work**, pointing the audience to your FAQs handout.
- Recap districting as an **opportunity at an acceptable price** for doing great things together.
- Make it so that to miss this chance would be a **misfortune** for one and all. We will realistically have this one chance to create a district, but other forces will keep coming without let or hindrance.
- Declare this moment a **celebration** our civic purpose, of who we are as friends and neighbors coming together for the sake of ourselves and each other.

Conclude with our mantra (chapter 6): That you know our neighbors, and know that happily there is enough abundant goodwill and good sense among us to make the district *possible* and enough of the opposite— here and there—to make it *necessary*. Pause. Let it sink in. Then say, "Questions?"

THE QUESTION AND ANSWER SESSION

Now for the fun part.

The Q&A isn't something to be endured until you can head for the side door. It's where you're going to do your best work, outpoint your opponents, and win over the undecided takers.

Knowing that the Q&A is coming enables us to discipline our opening presentation. We can focus on what we want to say, say it briefly, and stop. We know that if we get the broad brushstrokes right, there will be time enough in the Q&A to sketch in the details.

This makes us look good. We are masters of our material. We gain credibility by speaking directly to the audience and looking them in the eye. We are capable of delivering a lean and simple message—no complicating, hard to remember "ifs, ands, and buts"—so we won't have to read it.

Minimizing our presentation and maximizing the time we allow for Q&A will help assure takers, who are willing to listen and be persuaded, that their opinions are heard and their questions are answered.

Breakers—our more resolute opponents—are different. We enter the Q&A inviting them to declare themselves. They will come hoping to use comment time to skewer our influence among the takers. None of this surprises us. As we'll see in the next chapter we know exactly what they're doing and where they're heading.

Being prepared for all challenges, we don't have to control the agenda and dominate the meeting. We can open the floor to our opponents and let them have their say. Because we do this confidently and welcomingly, we show ourselves to be tolerant, responsive, and settled. This will impress undecided fence-sitters and policy makers alike.

But the Q&A isn't just our questioners' time. We're going to use our responses to lay out all the other finer points of our case that we've held in reserve until then. Thus the Q&A becomes just an extension of our own presentation, part of our plan.

The more our critics accuse us from the floor, the higher the drama of the exchange will be and the more attentive our listeners. In this situation, the folks who are still undecided will naturally begin to pick sides and establish loyalties. We'll see to it that they come our way.

Rome wasn't built in a day. We can't expect to win all the support we need in this one meeting either. Others will be needed, and we'll be in this contest for the long haul. But then I'm sure you knew that already.

$\mathcal{FAQ}_s$: Frequently Asked Questions

Good morning, Mr. Phelps. Your mission is . . .

—*Mission Impossible*

. . . to find a way to keep our community meetings from getting bogged down in details.

As we saw in our last chapter, many of our undecided neighbors— the takers—will want straight answers to questions of fact. So what's the problem? If you know enough to answer them, you also know that almost every answer is loaded with technical details. But not everybody is interested in every question, and hardly anyone wants to hear everything that you might think they should know.

The solution? You and your committee should put together a handout of frequently asked questions—FAQs. Work up succinct answers to likely questions. Pass them out at your community meetings. You can then give short verbal responses while referring questioners to more complete answers in hand. This also works for those folks who've missed your answers at previous meetings.

CHAPTER SEVENTEEN

THE QUESTIONS

Work with your preservation specialist, contact preservation organizations, and go online to develop your own answers to the following questions. Then decide which ones to put in your FAQs handout.

Keep the others in reserve for rapid response if you need them. Put all of them on our website, too, and update the list as needed. Just don't expect everyone to have access to it.

And, no, I haven't abandoned you here. Questions are always harder to identify than answers. If you haven't studied up enough to provide your own answers, then you're not ready for the Q&A. Divide the research among your committee members and share your answers. You'll appreciate the exercise when each of you has mastered what you'll all be responsible for in public.

One of the fine attributes of the preservation community is the general willingness of people to let you borrow text from their own materials. As always, be cautious about copyrights. But I think you'll find a lot of help out there when you go looking for it.

THE FAQS

So as *Dragnet*'s Sgt. Joe Friday might say, here are "the FAQs, nothing but the FAQs."

1. What is a local historic district?
2. How is a district designated?
3. What are the benefits to me of designation?
4. What is historically significant about our community?
5. What is the legal basis for a local historic district?
6. Does district designation affect my property rights?
7. Why isn't zoning sufficient to protect historic properties?

8. What is a zoning overlay?
9. What is the difference between a contributing and a non-contributing property?
10. What are design guidelines? How are they applied?
11. What does "historic integrity" mean?
12. How does designation affect my property values and taxes?
13. What is the HPC?
14. Will designation prevent me from repairing, altering, renovating, or adding on to my property?
15. What projects need approval?
16. How does the certificate of approval (appropriateness) process work?
17. How are HPC decisions enforced?
18. What if the HPC denies my application? How do I appeal?
19. Are there extra costs and fees associated with district designation?
20. Does district designation require me to fix up my house?
21. Is there money available to help preserve old buildings?
22. Will the HPC tell me what color to paint my house?
23. Can I make my building more energy efficient?
24. Will designation mean that new construction has to be designed a certain way?
25. Will interiors be subject to review?
26. What about demolition?
27. Will the district be expanded to cover more properties?

As we'll see next, not everyone will ask questions so mildly. Our most aggressive opponents will phrase them as pointed challenges. So I think it's time for us to learn to think politically about questions and answers, don't you?

EIGHTEEN

Thinking Politically about Q&A: The Moving Pattern of Opponents' Challenges

Our foes will provide us with arms.

—Virgil, *Aeneid*

Districting campaigns are hard to win. But they are easily lost in the give-and-take of open community forums where we take to the floor to respond to questions.

There is a pattern in our opponents' questions where the ground shifts with every answer—a pattern that is logical and predictable. Learn this pattern now and you'll know your adversaries' plans before they do themselves. Master it and you'll perform to peak capacity in the Q&A.

POLITICAL THEATER

Imagine what it'll be like. You recognize your first questioner, hear the question, and then begin an answer. You owe the questioner a response, yet you can't ignore everybody else. So you look around the room and . . . do you know what hits you? You realize that they *might be listening* for your answer, but they *sure are watching* to see how you do.

This is public theater. Performance counts as much as the substance of what is said. Each speaker is judged by a critical and skeptical audience.

Of course you'd better know your lines. You must be prepared to answer any question about preservation, or know when to ask a specialist to step in for you.

But don't think your critics pose every question to get an explanation from you. You'll need to recognize when a question isn't just a question but a challenge thrown down by your adversaries— a challenge which you can learn to pick up and skillfully use to your advantage.

UNDERSTANDING QUESTIONS

Listen to questions two ways. Ask yourself:

1. *What does the questioner want to know?* This is how we usually hear questions because we're thinking about responding with facts and explanations.
2. *Why, and how, is the question being asked?* If we are politically alert listeners, each question adds to our understanding of how the political dynamic of the designation process is shaping up.

We often miss this second way of thinking.

TYPES OF QUESTIONERS

Two types of questioners provide us with political opportunities.

1. **Takers**, who are our *unconvinced but convincible* questioners. They typically pose questions for clarification as they decide for or against districting.
2. **Breakers**, who are our *committed opponents.* They ask questions or make challenging statements to sway opinion against us.

Unlike us, breakers aren't responsible for a cogent plan, nor are they bound by fact or logic. They have an immediate advantage: the tendency of takers toward inaction when confronted by a confusion of counterclaims and irreconcilable differences. What you and I might call an unhelpful, uninformed, or ignorant question is often for breakers the smart political move.

DETECTING THE DIFFERENCE

You can usually distinguish between these two types of questioners by the way they pose their questions:

1. **Takers** typically ask *substantive* questions. For example, "What is involved in obtaining a certificate of approval [C of A]?" This is an open invitation for us to tell them more. It's a chance for us to get our message across, and they'll let us know when they've heard enough.
2. **Breakers** pose *rhetorical* questions. "Why would anybody want an additional layer of government?" For them, the question is the message, their policy statement. They aren't

seeking a convincing answer, and they are never satisfied with our response.

If you're not sure whether you're being led on by the first question a person asks, listen to the follow-up. Takers will typically ask for more detail: "Will I have to pay a fee for a C of A?" Breakers, however, will become more combative: "Isn't this a burden on the elderly?"

THE LIMITED ROLE OF ISSUES

So the question-and-answer format is deceiving. It sure looks like an invitation to serious policy discussion—well, at least until you get into it.

1. Questions asked by unconvinced takers are *opportunities* to advance our policies openly and fully. This is where advocacy as persuasive education plays its role and issues are important. Many conversations are ongoing. Your job is to establish a position and keep to it, reaffirming basic points and elaborating them as needed.
2. Our opponents' questions are *challenges* to be finessed and seized for the advantages they offer. Here political perspectives must rule and your responses should be politically calibrated.

One perspective stands above all others when it comes to dealing with breakers: this is not a *contest of issues using reasoned arguments as weapons*, but a *contest for influence using issues as weapons*. The issues they choose are the weapons we will use to defeat them.

ANTICIPATING OPPOSITION STRATEGY

I'm not claiming that breakers are actually conscious of the way they try to manipulate the Q&A to maximize their influence. It's enough that they *act* like they understand it.

Fortunately for us, their questions are driven by a political logic into a predictable pattern of arguments that offers us a ready-made strategy. When we learn to recognize this pattern, we are able to anticipate *what* they will argue, and generally *when*, before they know it themselves. Of course, if they're no good at this game, then so much the better for us.

HOW IT TYPICALLY BEGINS

The first move is to us. The historic district is our plan. We set the agenda. When we begin with advocacy, our emphasis is on historic preservation with the *historic* part—the valued legacy—emphasized.

Our opponents see districting in terms of historic *preservation*— that is, protection—but protection *from whom?* They take offense presuming we mean from them and they attack us for it. From there the pattern unfolds predictably.

OUTLINE OF THE MOVING PATTERN OF OPPONENTS' CHALLENGES

The pattern flows forward from a charge that preservationists don't trust property owners with their property, and it ends up arguing that it's preservationists who shouldn't be trusted with authority. In between lies an unfolding argument that appears in debate as a series of pointed questions or challenging statements.

There's a *pivotal shift* at the center of these questions around which everything turns. It occurs when opponents stop talking about historic preservation and start talking about property rights. If you listen closely, you'll hear that the arguments on either side of the shift evolve in a mirror image of each other.

Here's the basic outline of our opponents' moving line of attack using simple questions as examples.

Part One: Denying Historic Districting

1. **Arguments alleging our distrust of them.**
   Basic point: The district is personally demeaning.
   "Why don't you trust us with our property?"
2. **Arguments against the need for districting protection.**
   Basic point: Historic resources are already sufficiently protected.
   "Isn't this why we have zoning laws?"
3. **Arguments against the desirability of districting protection.**
   Basic point: The district will have undesirable consequences.
   "Why create a district that will lower property values?"
4. **Arguments against historic merit.**
   Basic point: History isn't and can't be the reason for districting.
   "Whaddya' mean historic? George Washington didn't sleep here, did he?"

THE PIVOTAL SHIFT: FROM HISTORIC PRESERVATION TO PROPERTY RIGHTS

Part Two: Affirming Property Rights

1. **Arguments for property rights merit.**
   Basic point: Property rights are sufficient reason for opposing districting.

"You're violating my personal property rights!"
2. **Arguments for the desirability of property rights protection.**
Basic point: Property rights have consequences more desirable than preservation.
"I have a right to the highest and best use of my property."
3. **Arguments for the need for property rights protection.**
Basic point: Property rights are about to be lost to districting.
"The district's a done deal!"
4. **Arguments affirming their distrust of us.**
Basic point: The district is a power grab by preservationists.
"These people can't be trusted with this kind of power!"

Read over this outline until you get a sense of the flow of changing questions and challenges. We'll be looking at each of these parts in greater detail in the following chapters.

A SMORGASBORD

OK, I know what you're thinking: I must be delusional to claim I know exactly how the debate will unfold. And so I would be, *if* I were saying that. But I'm not.

Instead, I want you to think of a smorgasbord—an open buffet that has a rich variety of dinner items laid out on a long table and arranged in a natural and predictable order, from appetizers to desserts. Now substitute the categories of questions for the variety of foods and you'll begin to see how I say questioning is predictable.

At a smorgasbord diners are free to select items in whatever order they choose. If we watch them, and anticipate that sooner or later they will eat a complete and balanced meal, we will not be surprised if they pick here among desserts, there at salads, now at the meats, and later at the vegetables. Wherever they start, we see with increasing clarity where they will move next as opportunities for making new selections diminish. You can bet on it.

CATCHING THE PIVOTAL SHIFT

Our answers to their questions drive the changing selections. In Part I we respond that district designation is about prudence not personalities, that it supplements zoning laws, and that government has a legitimate interest in protecting all kinds of historic resources and that preservation is indeed our central goal.

Because we have good preservation answers for every challenge, our opponents need to shift the focus of debate. The Q&A pivots when they declare, "This isn't about preservation. This is a property rights issue!" And so Part II unfolds.

PROPERTY RIGHTS AS POWER

The predictive pattern that I've outlined draws upon experience for its particulars and upon the logic of power for its organization.

Preservation is our primary goal, though it has other desirable results for us. But our adversaries see property rights mainly as an instrument—not an end—that enables them to do, or not to do, other things. Thus for them the property rights issue is about power or—in contemporary lingo—empowerment.

This political insight helps us stay focused on what we established in chapter 10. The contest isn't about the merits of *preservation* as much as it's joined where property interests collide with preservation over *districting*, for it's here that local law redefines the prerogatives of property ownership.

POLITICS NOT PRESERVATION

So we can't expect our adversaries to listen to us. They'll hear the points we advocate for preservation only to sidestep them. To do otherwise would be to arrest the momentum of their own necessary strategy.

They have no real choice but to ignore or misrepresent what we say about preservation *in order to get to the pivotal shift to construct their own symmetrically opposite defense of property rights against districting.*

That, in short, is the political logic of their situation.

Without this insight we're reduced to waiting to see what happens in the Q&A and improvising. With it we can seize their hostile questions and comments and make them part of our own strategic plan for defeating them while building a new sense of community with takers.

NINETEEN

Our Reframing Q&A Strategy

> He must be very ignorant, for he answers every question he is asked.
>
> —Voltaire

Let's look more closely now at how we'll respond to our opponents' questions in community meetings. Coming from our dyed-in-the-wool adversaries—called breakers—these challenges are aimed at blocking our efforts to win over undecided takers—those folks in the middle who are still making up their minds.

Breaker challenges may be posed as either questions or flat statements. I'll call all of them questions because each ends with the unspoken interrogative: "What do you say to *that*?"

OUR REFRAMING STRATEGY

We don't have to take the bait. We can decide how we want to "hear" the question and respond to it. We can answer it directly if it suits us. Often we'll reframe the question, taking a different angle that advances our message, not theirs, while still allowing us to be responsive. We don't want to get too deep into the weeds of their point of view.

Our Q&A strategy is simple and straightforward. We're not going to respond to our critics on their terms, much less argue with them. We'll answer them in ways designed to win over takers in the middle ground and isolate our critics. This is a key part of our plan to build a vital sense of community in the midst of conflict and use it to defeat our opponents. Here's my format for the next two chapters:

- I'll state a typical question and follow it with a brief interpretative comment.
- I'll suggest either a direct answer or a way of reframing the question and responding.
- Final comments are meant to help you see the larger context out of which our initial response emerges and point you toward a fuller response if it's needed.

Your sense of the moment will tell you whether to reframe or directly rebut a challenge to stop it in its tracks.

THINKING FLEXIBLY

There's no one right answer to any question. Keep your antennae up to gauge the sense and direction of the meeting. A small, relatively friendly meeting invites one kind of response while a large, highly contentious one requires another.

I've composed my examples for the more difficult but not outlandishly hostile meeting. It's up to you to gear them up or tone them down as you think best.

Remember that the unfolding pattern of questions exists only in the abstract. Breakers will be asking the questions they want to ask whenever they want to ask them.

That's why you can prepare but you can't really plan for the Q&A. Think strategically, where discussion can turn on a different axis with each question posed and each response given.

Each meeting can have its own direction, too. One might be dominated by procedural issues and another by challenges to historic merit.

This is where our moving pattern gives you an advantage. When we've been through a difficult meeting, our natural tendency is to prepare to refight it with better answers at the next meeting. That's probably wise, but it's likely that you'll have to deal with a whole new set of questions next time. These chapters can help you focus in on them by a process of elimination.

SURPRISE QUESTIONS

We want to reduce your uncertainty, yet some of the best questions are surprises. "My neighbor's husband died and the house and Social Security are all she has now. She wouldn't come here today, she's so upset. What do you say to her?"

You look around the room and you realize this is it: the one you didn't anticipate. The one that can lose it for you. The widow maker.

It takes you to the heart of what you know and think and want others to understand. When you can answer it with confidence and compassion and get a nod from the questioner, then you know you've passed the public test.

The only way to prepare for the unexpected is to practice and practice again answering questions you think you might get asked. Somewhere in the seams of the responses you develop you'll find just what you need when the time comes. So let's get started.

TWENTY

Answering Opposition Questions I: From "Distrust of Them" to the "Pivotal Shift"

Enemies are so stimulating.

—Katherine Hepburn

To recap: There are dozens of challenges that districting opponents across the country employ so regularly that we may treat them as inevitable. They can take the form of questions or challenging statements, but they are always argumentative.

Our opponents—the breakers—will toss these arguments at us one at a time, jumping from one topic to another. But what appears to be random is actually rooted in an orderly progression of challenges.

The pattern has two main components linked by a pivotal shift of focus. The first attacks historic districting and the second affirms the sanctity of private property rights.

We'll begin here by considering breakers' questions under the four headings of the first part that lead logically to the symmetrically unfolding second part in the next chapter:

- Arguments Alleging Our Distrust of Them.
- Arguments against the Need for Districting Protection.
- Arguments against the Desirability of Districting Protection.
- Arguments against Historic Merit.

I've selected the following core arguments—that is, some of the most common questions and challenges—from a longer list I've developed for classes and training programs. You're sure to hear their substance, if not the same phrasing angled the same way, in your own Q&A.

This selection is designed to get you thinking. Treat what I say as suggestions—examples—only.

PART ONE. DENYING HISTORIC DISTRICTING

A. Arguments Alleging Our Distrust of Them

1. **They say: *Why don't you trust us with our property?***

    Breakers like to portray themselves as victims. They're saying if we, personally, trusted our neighbors, personally, to be good citizens then we wouldn't be pressing this on them.

    They want takers to feel the same way. "Houstonians are being told they lack any right—even the smarts—to determine the appearance of their property," an opponent writes.[1] Variations include any claim that "they" will "tell me," "make me," or won't "let me" do this, that or the other. As a Santa Monica homeowner puts it, "They just want to decide what's best for us."[2]

    Reframe: *Why did we call this meeting today?*

We respond: *Because we know that all of us care about our community. We believe that there is enough trust and confidence among us, neighbor to neighbor, to do this extraordinary thing for each other. Make no mistake: We're either going to have the community we earn by working together—or the one we deserve by failing to act. Right now we could use your support for the kind of community we need. So, what do you say?*

We're holding out a welcoming hand to takers, asking for their help. And we're putting breakers on the spot: put up or shut up. This offer of empowerment is our antidote to their claims of victimhood.

2. **They say:** *Why didn't you ask us first?*

Snubbed, that's how they feel. Bypassed, overlooked, taken for granted. Some mean it; for others it's just an incitement.

Direct answer: *Suppose we had called a meeting as soon as the idea popped into our heads. Would you have approved a vague notion then? Or would you have told us to go away until we had a real proposal? We thought the latter. So today is the real beginning. Nothing's been decided—except that we'd like you to join us.*

Because breakers can't agree to join us, they insist the district isn't needed. The next section follows predictably.

B. **Arguments against the Need for Districting Protection**

1. **They say:** *If you trust us then why do we need more rules and regulations?*

This "if not . . . then" tactic tries to trap us in a contradiction, or an irrelevancy. "Where's the crisis?" we're asked in Camden, South Carolina. And in Evanston, Illinois: "We don't have people making stupid changes to their homes. A preservation district is unnecessary."[3]

Direct answer: *This isn't about you or me in particular. It's about how we can secure our community's future. Only by* *trusting each other today can we provide for tomorrow. And so we trust you'll join us in supporting the district.*

That's the way to avoid finger-pointing. It's different, of course, if you have a real crisis or gathering storm that's pushing your effort. Maybe there's no crisis now, but as a Floridian put it, "we don't know who will come in the future."[4]

2. **They say: *Isn't this why we have zoning laws?***

As a Maine opponent asks, "Why do we need more ordinances when the old ordinances have been working?"[5] Zoning laws are said to provide ample and fair protection for all property owners, including preservationists. Breakers want takers to feel we're asking a lot for no reason or little advantage.

Reframe: *What will districting do for us that zoning laws can't?*

We respond: *It will protect us against identity theft.*

Each of us is invested, personally and financially, in our neighborhood, which has its own identity that *we value* and *gives us value in return.* Without the district overlay, zoning alone can't protect the community's historical integrity and distinctive character.

Zoning allows a wide variety of structures and landscaping without considering the unique character and needs of a particular area. As zoning changes, so do development standards. District designation still permits rezoning, but it establishes a constant set of development standards unique to the district that won't change with rezoning. The district will promote healthy change consistent with the visual character of our community.

Use this rule of thumb: The louder the defense of zoning the more the advocate (a) wants to introduce incompatible change and (b) believes that the district will in fact afford real protections to the community.

3. They say: *The free market can decide what's valuable and worth preserving.*

Districting isn't needed, critics argue, because the free market—which shows what people value by what they will pay for—is a more reliable indicator of what should be saved and how. Breakers may argue it, but they don't really care what the market says about preservation. They simply don't want anyone—not only preservationists—telling them what to do.

The market argument is a ready-made inducement for takers to stop listening. When they're perplexed by choices, it's a relief to be told that the supposed automatic mechanism of the marketplace can take over. We need to shift their attention from theory to practice without, however, coming across as anti-free marketers. That would be politically stupid.

Reframe: *As a smart investor, don't you want to manage your risk?*

We respond: *Look, we're not indifferent property investors here. We don't care more for some abstract market theory than for how the market actually treats us. The historic district will give us greater security of investment, when the historic setting of each property is well maintained. There is a robust market for preservation nationally, and our purpose is to foster its ability to operate here to the advantage of all of us.*

There isn't just one market, and not all markets are equal. Without historic districting, property markets focus on short-term results at the expense of valuing the long-term benefits of historic preservation. Landlords in rental markets will damage buildings to maximize net operating income by avoiding maintenance or making harmful repairs and alterations. Long-term homeowners rarely have more than an abstract concern for the economic consequences of what they do to their properties. New building contractors in the redevelopment market will read the economic tea leaves in favor of teardowns.

Built-in market correctives don't operate here, either. Once historic resources are lost through bad decisions, they can never be recouped and the damage done to the rest of us can't be repaired. As Indiana homeowner association volunteer John Tousley puts it, once historic resources vanish, "we become just another place on the map."[6] Regulation in these circumstances isn't antimarket. Districting keeps historic capital in play, ownership in private hands, and the market for historic properties fully operating.

As we move through defending the need for districting, our opponents will start focusing on its alleged limits and liabilities.

C. Arguments against the Desirability of Districting Protection
1. They say: *You can't stop change.*

This seems obvious to those who believe that preservation means shrink-wrapping communities or freezing them in time. One of my favorite examples is, "If Manitou Springs had a historic district when the town was created, we'd all be living in teepees." A more sophisticated challenge is that we will derail progress without, however, achieving preservation.

Reframe: *Change is certain, progress isn't and [expletive deleted] happens.*

We respond: *Let's go for rooted growth and real progress—not random, risky change.*

Watch your adjectives and verbs. Don't talk about "*managed* growth" or "*directing* change." It sounds like you've decided what people ought to want.

That's why I prefer to speak of assuring "rooted growth." We encourage growth that respects the past, and we welcome new choices that stimulate growth in the local economy and improve our quality of life. That's real progress and preservation is an inseparable part of the process.

2. **They say: *But design is so subjective! Who can say what good taste is?***

We could talk all day about the problem of "good taste." Design review isn't at all about what we "like" or "dislike." That would be justifiable cause for complaint. Instead, the HPC looks for a project's compatibility with its setting in terms of recognized standards made locally more specific through design guidelines. Explaining this will get you only so far. There will be some listeners who are in thrall of a deep relativism that's skeptical about the very existence of dependable standards or anyone's *ability* or *right* to make decisions based on them. The best way to reach everyone else is by commonsense analogy.

Reframe: *Do you know the difference between an author and an editor?*

We respond: *Editors don't write the books; editors make them better. And what makes a good editor? The ability to help a writer choose what works best. For us, the question isn't how anyone can know what makes a good book. It's whether we want a good read. The role of the HPC in design review is very much like that. No doubt about it: the process helps owners make good choices. The real question is whether they want a good result.*

There's a big difference between being *subjective* and being *arbitrary*. Every day, democracies make decisions about what's subjective—such as what's ethically right and wrong—and then we make laws and establish procedures to see to it that our decisions aren't applied arbitrarily.

3. **They say:** *Preservation is just too expensive!*

   Variation: *I have a right to do what I prefer and can afford.* Bear in mind that those who oppose districting always inflate preservation-related costs, and they'll find contractors who'll arm them with worse-than-worst case scenarios.

   Reframe: *Do you remember the car service commercial, "You can pay me* now—*or you can pay me* later"?

   We respond: *Valuable properties like ours become just old buildings when they lose the integrity of compatible materials and design details. Substituting inexpensively is like taking part of the principal of your investment and throwing it away. Today the smart money is on preserving older properties intact. And the surprising thing is that over time, investing in preservation is cost-effective.*

   Good design and construction will enhance the district, which, in turn, will lend its prestige to the security of our investments. There may be opportunity costs in building for prestige, but there are costs incurred if owners make inappropriate changes that detract from their own and their neighbors' properties. As Edmund Burke said, "Mere parsimony is not economy. . . . Expense, and great expense, may be an essential part of true economy."

   Preservationist Jeremy Wells in Philadelphia gives Burke's point a modern phrasing: "The cheap quick fix is often the most costly fix in the long run."[7] HPCs are open to proposals that are both appropriate and financially reasonable for property owners. Responsible repair and maintenance of older buildings can be an additional expense, as can appropriate renovations and new construction. But higher initial costs are generally compensated by stronger revenues and property values.

4. **They say:** *The historic district will lead to lower property values when I go to sell!*

"Historic district zoning," a North Carolinian claims, "reduces the number of potential buyers by eliminating those who do not want their property subject to the historic district bureaucracy; fewer buyers means lower prices."[8]

This argument is appealing in theory, but baseless in fact. Many realtors emphasize historic district locations. Urban districts may also be marketed for their scale and compactness, walkability and convenience to shopping, churches, and schools—all aspects of contemporary lifestyle preferences.

Reframe: *Why are realtors so eager to list historic district properties?*

We respond: *Properties in historic districts frequently— even substantially—outperform sales of similar properties elsewhere. Where values are declining, preservation stabilizes them. Preservation sells, and not just because some buyers appreciate historic settings. Buyers are aware that a historic district signifies the presence of a whole mix of positive factors— social, economic, political, and cultural—that make living or working there desirable. They recognize the stability and strength of property values, too. The free market has demonstrated that people will pay a premium to buy property in sheltered communities, whether in historic districts or in gated suburban developments.*

Don't be cowed by studies purporting to prove us wrong. Stick to your guns—and to documentation available through your State Historic Preservation Office and the National Trust. Tony Felice, preservation officer for Mesa, Arizona, says that creating districts is "a slam dunk in terms of economic development. When a home is designated as historic, we've seen an increase in property values from 30 to 35%, often without even doing anything to the house."[9] Don't be surprised if such statements get your critics to do a 180° turn and hit you on the alleged consequences of rising property values.

5. **They say: *I'm not going anywhere, so this'll just raise my property taxes, won't it?!***

   Taxes—a great bugbear of American politics. Challenge their perspective.

   Reframe: *Is there anyone present who'd like to buy property that's guaranteed to lose value and lower our taxes?*

   We respond: *I thought so. For most of us, our property is our biggest investment for the future. A higher selling price for a neighbor's house is never bad news.*

   District designation itself isn't a direct factor in property tax rates or appraisals. Owners might also qualify for tax advantages in the district as their net worth expands—but don't oversell this possibility. Your state or local preservation adviser should be able to speak briefly to the tax issue and explain credits.

6. **They say: *Rising values will change the neighborhood for the worse!***

   Issues vary. A common charge is gentrification that transforms older communities into chic enclaves for the rich or quaint mini-Mayberrys or tourist destinations. Then there are predictions that districting will displace low-income residents, put pressures on ethnic diversity, keep out young homeowners, and increase financial burdens on working families and the elderly. Just whose culture, some ask, is to be preserved?

   This speculative chumming hopes to draw in takers and hook them on being victims, too. Yet it's actually one of our best openings for challenging takers to join with us to take responsibility for the future.

   Reframe: *How can we be sure that the district will do what we want it to do?*

   We respond: *By everybody working together instead of just criticizing. The district is a tool. Let's fit it to our pur-*

poses. All we're saying is, let's be proactive about the kind of community that we—all of us—want to maintain, instead of just letting things happen. Doing nothing is far more likely to lead where none of us wants to go.

What issues are you facing? Have you handled them in your practical vision for districting? As for gentrification: The wealthy—like the poor—are always with us. Do we want them isolated in suburban developments? Isn't it better to lure them to a diverse historic district, where they'll contribute to the tax base, provide money for civic projects, develop sensitivity for urban issues, and join in local affairs as socially conscious and responsible citizens?

Historic districts can be democratic about who gets what. With the visibility that districting gives us at City Hall we can work for tax policy and other considerations to help maintain diversity and homeownership. Everyone in a district benefits from investment, not just folks in grand homes or businesses with political pull.

With the advantages of districting defended, the breakers move on to attack the historic merit of our proposal.

D. Arguments against Historic Merit

Breakers portray our choices in zero-sum terms, a kind of Newton's Third Law of Motion applied to public policy: an advance in any one policy direction necessitates an equal and opposite retreat in all others.

Thus when we say we're for preservation, they tell takers that our plan will cost them dearly. But as soon as we assert economic benefits, they conclude that we can't be serious about preservation.

They see preservation, then, as smoke and mirrors used to screen some other goal entirely. What that end might be isn't as important to them as pointing out that our claim to base the district on historic merit is a sham.

1. **They say:** *This isn't really about historic preservation at all, is it? It's about property values, commercial investment, tourism—it's just about the money!*

    Variation #1: *It's about lifestyle preferences, not preservation.*

    Variation #2: *It's antigrowth. Preservation is the excuse.*

    Variation #3: *It's about taste, the snobbish enforcement of an elitist aesthetic.*

    Variation #4: *It's about . . .* virtually any other interest *except* genuine preservation.

    Breakers want to paint us as liars or cheats who will manipulate authentic preservation values for our own selfish purposes. Our response will be to deny their zero-sum perspective and replace it with a positive affirmation that there are net gains for interests that are important to takers.

    Reframe: *How do we know when preservation is working?*

    We respond: *When it saves a legacy, puts smiles on people's faces and money in their pockets. Preservation isn't just old buildings standing around. If homes aren't enjoyable, neighborhoods livable, and businesses profitable, then folks aren't going to invest in preservation. There's no hidden agenda here! What you see is what you get.*

    We want takers to see that districting is a win-win situation for everybody across the board, except those who would profit at the expense of the rest of us. In its consequences preservation is democratic, not elitist.

    The only response available to breakers is to deny outright that there is anything worth preserving.

2. **They say:** *Whaddya' mean, historic? George Washington didn't sleep here, did he?*

    We first ran into this gag line in chapter 1. Its counterpart from Newnan, Georgia, is, "No tour bus is ever going to drive down this street!"

Variation: Critics claim that while maybe a few historic properties exist, *"There's not enough all together to justify a whole district!"*

This will make sense to takers because most folks have a mountaintop view of history. They see only those events and places that have risen above the lower hills and valleys of the past where our own local legacy was built.

One of the things that we preservationists do well, given time, is open people's eyes to the history in their midst. The problem for us is not to be condescending.

Reframe: *[Jokingly.] The past just isn't what it used to be, is it?*

We respond: *Well, at least not the big-event way we all used to think about it in American History class. We're not pulling a fast one here. The district has to satisfy rigorous standards under law before it may be designated historic by the City Council.*

This is our opportunity to have our preservation specialist—or a SHPO representative—explain "historic" as a concept and clear up confusion over the criteria used for determining contributing properties.

3. **They say:** *Well, my property isn't historic! It should be excluded!*

This expression of narrow self-interest signals that breakers are at their wits' end in attacking districting from a historic preservation angle. Their hope is that takers will see the unfairness of the plan.

Reframe: *Let's cut to the chase. What you really want to know is why we don't make the district voluntary, right?*

We respond: *Because it's bad public policy. Yes, districting is about zoning policy. But people don't just opt out of zoning arrangements because they want to. Talk about fairness! That would amount to spot rezoning and policy nullification*

*by personal fiat. And where would that leave the rest of us?!
As Ben Franklin said, "We either hang together or we hang
separately." We've made a legitimate case for bringing all
properties into the district fold, and the courts say it's constitutional for the City to include them.*

Our affirmation of districting's constitutionality brings
differences to a head and it's here that debate pivots. Breakers shift their focus from attacking districting on preservation grounds to blocking designation in defense of property
rights.

NOTES

1. Jim Saltzman, "Changes to Preservation Ordinance Threaten
Property Rights," www.preservationsanity.org, 1999.

2. Clara Sturak, "Historic District Opponents Rally," www.smmirror
.com, *Santa Monica Mirror*, March 13–19, 2005.

3. Jane Adler, "Preservation Haul," www.chicagotribune.com,
Chicago Tribune Online Edition, December 28, 2003.

4. Jason Holland, "Hearing on Historic District Tonight," *Osceola
News-Gazette*, January 27, 2005.

5. Dennis Hoey, "Maquoit Bay: Property Rights vs. Preservation,"
www.meepi.org, *Portland Press Herald*, July 3, 2001.

6. Michelle Browning, "Nostalgic Zionsville Looks Back, Then
Ahead," www.thenoblesvilleledger.com, February 22, 2005.

7. "Letters: A Historic District Offers Various Benefits," www.dfw
.com, *Philadelphia Inquirer*, July 1, 2002.

8. Mark Binker, "Westerwood Residents Split on Plan," *Greensboro
News and Record*, January 21, 2002.

9. Lisa Selin Davis, "Historic Preservation: Finding Room for History in the Desert," www.Americancity.org, The Next American City,
Inc., 2004.

TWENTY-ONE

Answering Opposition Questions II: From the "Pivotal Shift" to "Distrust of Us"

> Hmmm. . . . What am I doing here? I'm chasing that guy.
> . . . Uh, no. . . . He's chasing me!
>
> —Guy Pearce, *Memento*

It takes but a nanosecond for breakers to respond to our observation on the constitutionality of historic districts . . . and then they're off and gunning for us with an affirmative defense of property rights.

Passing through the pivotal shift, challenges in this chapter unfold through the following categories that are a mirror image of the preceding chapter:

- Arguments for Property Rights Merit.
- Arguments for the Desirability of Property Rights.
- Arguments for the Need for Property Rights Protection.
- Arguments Affirming Their Distrust of Us.

So take a deep breath. We're going to take pains to pay them the respect they deserve, which is to explain to takers, the fence-sitters, why our opponents are mistaken.

Don't show impatience. But never let their accusations hang in the air, either. He who hesitates is toast. You might not think much of your opponents' arguments, but remember what the elder George Bush once said: "It's no exaggeration to say that the undecideds could go one way or another."

THE PIVOTAL SHIFT

Breakers assert that just because the courts have ruled that historic districting is constitutional doesn't mean that (1) the judges are right or (2) that politicians should enact our proposal. We can pinpoint the pivot this way:

At the moment of the shift, breakers pull out their biggest gun and claim (BANG!) that this is nothing but "a grab for power!" "The issue here is control," a landowner says in Maine.[1] An Internet blogger sums up districting as a "land grab . . . to control property."[2] Breakers claim that the "grab" can come only with the violation of their freedom to exercise basic constitutional property rights.

Makers say:
THE CONSTITUTION PERMITS
HISTORIC DISTRICTING.

THE PIVOTAL SHIFT

Breakers say:
THE CONSTITUTION GUARANTEES
SUPERIOR PROPERTY RIGHTS.

They operate under what I call the Law of Inverse Proof. When we point out that the courts don't find a conflict between districting and property rights, they claim that that fact itself proves their rights are in jeopardy. The courts may ignore property rights, they say, but it's the community's duty to honor and protect them. And once they assert that, the rest unfolds predictably.

PART TWO: AFFIRMING PROPERTY RIGHTS

A. Arguments for Property Rights Merit

1. They say: *You're violating my personal property rights!*

This change in direction can lead us down into the rabbit warren of constitutional theory and ideological conflict, as we'll see in the next chapter. How much of this kind of talk can the audience take? Our response should be quick, clean, and confident.

Direct answer: *Property rights aren't absolute, and everybody knows they don't trump our basic political rights— including our right as free citizens to make laws about property. The Founding Fathers knew that. The Constitution says historic districts are fine, according to the Supreme Court, and it's time we move on.*

As long as due process is assured, districting doesn't negate existing or invested property rights. Get a preservation law specialist to confirm the Supreme Court's line of interpretation since the 1978 Penn Central case. Breakers, of course, will have none of it, not when American civilization hangs by a paint chip.

2. They say: *No one should be able to tell me what to do with my property.*

"We must have the freedom to do what we want to do," a Michigan builder proclaims. Proportional judgment—the calculation of relative goods—vanishes at this point. A Florida couple opposed an entire district simply because it might have kept them from hanging a front door of their choice. The Reverend Lee A. Earl of an historic African American Baptist Church in Alexandria, Virginia, whose building plans were frustrated by preservation, proclaimed: "Slavery and oppression is not about chains. It is about buildings and dirt. . . . This is America! We have property rights we've suffered and died for."[3]

Variation #1: *I have a God-given right. . . .* It underscores the speaker's belief in the sanctity and absolute quality of this alleged right. But the subtext is always that the speaker's own human will to pursue any and every desire is inviolable.

Variation #2: *It's my money and I can do as I like.*

Variation #3: *You don't pay my property taxes, so don't tell me what to do.*

Reframe: *What are the three most important words we use when we talk about rights?*

We respond: *"As long as." Example: We may exercise our property rights as long as what we do doesn't adversely affect the rights of others. We use zoning laws to define how that works in practice, regardless of who pays for what, and districting is part of the zoning code.*

Zoning is long-established practice. The basic concept is that the government may restrict a property owner's right to use land in a way profitable to the owner but detrimental to surrounding properties. Zoning promotes appropriate uses in the *future*, and the historic district—which ties growth to the legacy of the *past*—will be a zoning overlay.

Specifically say that the HPC can't tell property owners how to use their properties or what to build on them. All the

HPC may do is decide that a style or alteration is incongruent based on the existing significant characteristics of the district. Thus HPC decisions are based on *findings of fact*, and not on the personal preferences of commissioners. A certificate of approval cannot be denied unless there is a finding of fact to back up the decision.

3. **They say:** *This is an invasion of privacy!*

   People will call "private" anything they're used to deciding on their own, even if it has public consequences. Thus accustomed to exercising property rights one way, they are unsettled by the feeling that the district will alter what has been a private matter. It's more about feelings of independence than rights.

   Direct answer: *It's out of respect for privacy that historic districts are silent about changes that take place within the walls of a property. But what happens outside, in public, can hardly be defined as private. The question of privacy hinges on your front door. Inside, you're the only one who has to live with your actions. Outside, everyone does.*

   Privacy has become a hot-button topic in recent years, and the courts have found a constitutional right to privacy in certain circumscribed, highly personal areas. Doing what we want with our property is *not* one of those areas. Still, some folks claim a right to a blanket freedom to do whatever they wish and then say that whatever goes on under it is private. That is a pernicious notion.

4. **They say:** *Real preservationists should preserve our traditional culture of liberty!*

   We will reserve this question for our next chapter where we'll be looking at historical claims and radical ideologies.

   From these arguments for the intrinsic value of property rights, breakers next turn to arguing that property rights are desirable because of what they prevent or secure.

B. Arguments for the Desirability of Property Rights

1. **They say:** *Why trade our rights for another layer of government?*

   This basic dislike of government is usually wrapped in the garb of property rights. Why should people vote "themselves into a control box they can never get out of," says a critic, and give up "those constitutional homeowner rights that make this country special for the average person?"[4] By defending property rights (but on specious constitutional grounds) breakers can justify their antipathy to government.

   Breakers often have a very shallow concept of government, seeing it only in terms of restraining freedom. But Jefferson affirmed in the Declaration of Independence that we freely create governments to do our bidding, to serve purposes that we join together to achieve. If we're optimistic about each other, then we expect that government assists our civilized cooperation far more than it jerks our chains. Jefferson clearly understood that good political institutions are a free people's gift to themselves.

   Reframe: *Would you deny us the right to empower ourselves as a community?*

   We respond: *The district's review procedures will give us real leverage whenever the government—or anyone else— starts making designs on us. Let's stop complaining about how the interests of average citizens are always ignored—by big government, big money, or big pains—and decide today, right now, to do something about it! HPC procedures are strong enough to assure us respect, but the actual regulations are considerably less complicated than you might think. Your support and participation can help guarantee that we get the mix right.*

   Do we want a community like Blanche DuBois in *A Streetcar Named Desire*, always dependent "on the kindness of strangers"? Texas state legislator Jessica Farrar says that "if residents don't drive their neighborhood, outside developers will."[5] An advocate in Tampa says that districting "increases neighborhood visibility with city officials" and another in Bloomington, Indiana, says it "creates an identifiable voice" in local affairs that gives a community a competitive advantage. New York City's Historic Districts Council calls itself "The Voice for Your Neighborhood." Designation also requires every federal agency, under Section 106 of the Historic Preservation Act of 1966, to take into account how any federally funded undertaking might affect our district.

2. **They say:** *I have a right to the highest and best use of my property.*

The argument—that we're denying owners the value in their land—depends on the propositions that (1) the value of one parcel is separable from the value of others, (2) the property owner has sole claim to it, and (3) the owner has an absolute right to the maximum return on investment. The affirmation of property rights carries the alleged promise of harvesting the largest profits from the land.

Reframe: *What is the three-word axiom of real estate?*

We respond: *"Location, location, location." Say what you will, common decency says it's just plain wrong to soak up value from your surroundings and not be considerate of others. Acceding to districting is but a small token of respect.*

Realtors who make a living off the value of property know that public and private contributions to the setting add value to a property. Historic settings are especially vulnerable to selfish grim reapers. Besides, much public investment—your tax dollars and mine—go into creating the infrastructure that creates part of a property's value. As for "highest and best use," the courts disagree while affirming

the lesser standard of a reasonable use and return on investment.

Because we remain unmoved by their arguments for the
preemptive desirability of preferring rights over districting,
breakers move on to assert that we have shown that property
rights need protecting.

C. Arguments for the Need for Property Rights Protection

This section contains a litany of procedural charges meant
to sway takers and public officials. No reframing here, these al-
legations must be met head-on and refuted.

1. They say: *The district's a done deal!*

Breakers claim that we're just going through the motions
of public meetings since the fix is in. This, they say, is a de-
nial of due process and a violation of their rights.

Direct answer: *[With humor.] Well now, that is good
news! Why am I always the last to know?! I thought we had a
good case, but I didn't know the City Council was in the bag.
I guess you won't have to attend the public hearings now.
We'll give 'em your regards.*

Of course, if the City Council is behind the initiative,
then you might want to make a more serious affirmation of
due process. But mild humor is the best way to handle a wild
conspiracy theory. That brings us to the next argument.

2. They say: *The district map has been gerrymandered to deny equal protection of my property rights.*

Variation: *The map has changed. How can a property be
historic one day be declared nonhistoric (or vice versa) the
next?*

The charge means to tell takers that the map is dishonest and that some properties have been included or excluded for inappropriate reasons.

Direct answer: *The map has been developed by the application of consistent criteria—which is to say by the knuckle-*

rappers who know the law and have kept everybody else's hands off of it! When it has been altered it has been in response to legitimate considerations.

The map's author—preferably backed up by a SHPO official—should briefly explain its rationale and how decisions were made.

3. **They say:** *The City's planning staff has colluded with proponents, thus using our tax dollars to support the violation of our property rights.*

The goal is to convince others that our opponents have been denied equal protection of the law or equal access to what rightfully belongs to everybody. It makes us look like we've been skulking around City Hall sticking our paws into the public till.

Direct answer: *The courts have found that supporting preservation through districting is a legitimate function of government. Staff members have provided professional assistance to us and anyone else who has asked, including opponents.*

You should have the City's chief planning officer or staff detail the scope of the department's work on the district.

4. **They say:** *The district study was biased by preconceptions about how it ought to turn out.*

The charge intends to cover a variety of sins from simple bias to ignoring facts to targeting specific properties for control.

Direct answer: *The study is no more or less biased than a diagnosis by a doctor who is looking for the facts and is determined to provide the best treatment. The district study has been professionally carried out and its recommendations follow its findings.*

Focus on the facts that justify districting. The specialist who did the survey should have a brief, persuasive response that avoids jargon and defensiveness.

---

5. **They say:** *Community meetings have been biased.*

This is a maddening complaint that is unreasonable on its face. Next they'll be claiming we were unfairly better organized than they, more articulate, and so forth.

Direct answer: *The truth is that bias in any meeting attaches to the better argument, the stronger facts, the clearer case. It's also true that we called this meeting to promote districting. But as evidenced by this extended Q&A, we're trying to give you every opportunity to state your feelings as well.*

Keep a detailed record of every opportunity opponents have for speaking out. If this charge becomes a serious issue, you might offer to hold an independently moderated joint meeting (see chapter 24). Whether it's held or not, the offer will be as good as gold if you have to defend yourself against having shown bias in your community hearings.

6. **They say:** *The proposal keeps changing on us.*

The suggestion is that we're trying to put something over on the community and can't be trusted.

Direct answer: *Changes are simply the proof you need that we're listening to you and revising in light of what we're hearing. Obviously, the district's not a done deal, now is it?*

Ask if they have any particular complaint and then explain the changes you've made.

7. **They say:** *There will be no end to the restrictions you'll impose. This is just the start.*

This kind of agitation plays up to folks who tend to feel powerless. Breakers are suggesting that designation will give the power elite the opening they need to roll back property rights.

Direct answer: *Guidelines may be expanded or shrunk in the future, depending on experience and what the community desires. As always, the best check on unwanted regula-*

tions is not to shy away from what needs to be done today, but to become involved so that the decisions will come from you.

Don't let them get away with such a counsel of fear. It's demeaning to our political legacy of citizen boards and citizen responsibility for historic districts.

As we move through defending what we've done procedurally, breakers begin to attack us personally for who they say we are, our qualifications, and what this means for the future.

D. Arguments Affirming Their Distrust of Us

1. They say: *The district is being rammed down our throats.*

This all-purpose procedural charge implies that we're pursuing designation in a damn-the-torpedoes full-speed-ahead fashion. The focus isn't on the ramming but the rammer.

Direct answer: *We've called this meeting and will have others so that the community will have time to deliberate carefully. We are exceeding the requirements of due process.*

Once again, go over the procedure so everyone knows how districting will move ahead.

2. They say: *Do you enjoy dividing the neighborhood?*

Breakers use this argument as a counterweight to our claim that we're pursuing districting with the good of the neighborhood in mind.

Reframe: *How can we get past this politics of blame? Surely no good can come of it.*

We respond: *Honest people can honestly disagree over issues. You don't have to make it personal. As responsible citizens, we have a duty to speak out on community issues. We're all united in that responsibility even though we might differ on policy. We shouldn't let anyone take advantage of it to drive us apart and mischaracterize what this is all about.*

Isn't it interesting that those who are most vocal about splitting the community are the least inclined to accept any community obligations beyond the pursuit of their own desires? If they persist, tell them you regret that they seem determined to go their own way, but that maybe Churchill was right: "A world united is better than a world divided; but a world divided is better than a world destroyed."

The truth is that property rightists are unsurpassed when it comes to alienating neighbor from neighbor. Our job is to see to it that they end up isolating themselves on the far edge of public opinion.

3. **They say: *These are wealthy, well-educated folks who look down on the rest of us.***

This is a transparent but potent playing of the class card and possibly an opaquely ethnic gamble as well.

Direct answer: *I don't mind lies being told about me. That's politics. But I hate inaccuracy. The truth is, I'm not that rich. [Alternatively: I'm not that educated.]*

Humor is always the best rejoinder to a scurrilous remark.

4. **They say: *Nobody elected these people. They've just appointed themselves to tell us what to do.***

We're the "taste police," "architectural Gestapo," "cultural tyrants," "preservation prigs"—insults so clever you might think they came from a distaff version of Cole Porter's "You're the Tops!"

Reframe: *Why would anybody volunteer for this kind of personal abuse?*

We respond: *Let me tell you, it takes a lot of fortitude to get up and do this when you figure someone's going to attack your character. But, you know what? Volunteerism—where ordinary folks like you and me stand up and do extraordinary things—is part of what has made this country great. If you're civic-minded and will join us, you'll see what I mean. If not, nothing I can say will make you any happier.*

"The community screams and shouts about a lack of leadership," says former HPC Chair Mary Cabell Eubanks in Greensboro, North Carolina. "Then it screams at those who take leadership."[6]

5. **They say:** *These people can't be trusted with this kind of power!*

It gets worse. Maybe you don't know it, but alleged HPC intimidation of property owners is "the same device that has been used effectively in East Germany, in Hitler's Germany, and in other similar societies in Europe, Bolshevik Russia, Red China" and now, the fellow who wrote those words warns us, in Russells Mills, Massachusetts.[7] Takes your breath away, doesn't it?

Direct answer: *I couldn't agree with you more. As James Madison said, "The truth is that all men having power ought to be mistrusted." But note: he didn't say that therefore no one should have power. When we do this thing, it's going to be done right. There will be the law that governs the HPC. There will be due process. And there will be all of us watching and participating. The active involvement of all is the best check on abuse by any. You're good to be cautious, but even better to be involved.*

More mundanely, point out that all HPC meetings will be open to the public, agendas posted, and commissioners nominated and approved by the City Council in open meetings. Explain that the HPC is not a lawmaking body, that it operates under rules of procedure, and that its decisions may be appealed. Note, too, that commissioners serve without compensation and recuse themselves in conflict-of-interest situations.

Remind takers that the alternative is to leave development to wholly unelected "self-appointed" interests—often a financial and commercial elite—whose only responsibility is to their bottom line, not the community.

If you find yourself targeted for a full ideological assault on government by property rightists, you're probably going to have to run a different kind of skirmish than our simple Q&A framework suggests. Our next chapter is designed to help you stand your ground when they roll out the really big guns.

NOTES

1. Dennis Hoey, "Maquoit Bay: Property Rights vs. Preservation," www.meepi.org, July 3, 2001.
2. Matt Neunke, "Historic Conflicts," home.comcast.net/~neoeugenics/historical, n.d.
3. *Washington Post*, December 18, 2004.
4. users.rcn.com/landgrab/summary, n.d.
5. Jessica Farrar, "Politics in Practice," www.archvoices.org, 2004.
6. *Greensboro News and Record*, March 21, 2002.
7. users.rcn.com/landgrab/summary, n.d.

TWENTY-TWO

Skirmishing with Radical Property Rightists

I was a lot more attractive when the evening began.

—Woody Allen, *Annie Hall*

"My home is my castle, not Kafka's," a critic says. Does that surprise you? Not the sentiment—it's common enough—but that he calls on Kafka?!

I'm impressed. It's a great line. There *is* more intelligence alight in our adversaries than we sometimes care to admit. Can appearances last? It's up to us to see that they don't.

A PROPERTY RIGHTS FIGHT

Let's suppose that our opponents in the Q&A aren't your typical neighbors or developers who simply don't like the district. Assume instead that they're as committed to private property rights as we are to preservation—possibly even more so. What if they have the single-mindedness of true radicals?

How does this change things? First off, they'll start at the pivotal shift and move straight into an aggressive affirmation—not merely a defense—of property rights. And they won't sit still, either, for any other Q&A on the need for, desirability, or merit of historic districting. They'll come at us again and again and hold on to their issue like a pit bull. In that case, we have two objectives:

1. First, to survive. We do this by beating back their attacks.
2. Then to sideline them. We do this by showing them to be politically unattractive.

The first is enough. The second is better. Lucky for us, local ideologues are often all too happy to oblige us.

THE LURE OF IDEOLOGY

Committed property rightists who aren't professional intellectuals are pretty much like the rest of us. They read whatever pleases them and is easy to get.

They surf the Internet for bloggers who share their passion. Much of the stuff you can find by Googling their issues is in the nature of smart-mouth manifestos and snide commentary. But not all of it. Some of it is very good—intelligent and defensible—and it travels well.

Roger Pilon of the Cato Institute in Washington, D.C., for example, has reasonably argued that our preferences for merely good things—such as preserving our architectural heritage—can never be rights in the same sense that we have a right to private property. Still, we can accept that distinction without adopting his conclusion in congressional testimony that "People may use their property in any way they wish, provided only that in the process they do not take what belongs free and clear to others."[1]

This, and a growing body of libertarian literature on property rights and "takings," is the heady stuff of big ideas. "For those who like this sort of thing," as Lincoln said, "this is the sort of thing they like."

Let's hope our local opponents like it a whole lot. If they make too much of it we can make a meal of them.

How so? Consider this: the property rights cause is for them what preservation is for us—a danger, if that's what they think politics is all about. The more they immerse themselves in these sophisticated legal and doctrinal defenses of rights, the less attentive they'll be to all those down-to-earth lessons about practical politics I've been talking about. And then we've got them.

So we want to encourage them to run with radical property rights. It's like judo. An opponent charging with abandon is more easily thrown. And no one is more politically reckless than the acolyte who quickens to the distant yoo-hoo of ideology.

AN UNWINNABLE DEBATE

Here's the situation: Pilon's argument is more the stuff of long-running constitutional law debates than of historic districting as you and I experience it. The players in his game are at the level of the Supreme Court and Congress, his Cato Institute and our National Trust for Historic Preservation. Down here, we play smaller ball in fewer innings.

You and I can't win a philosophical debate that pits radical property rights against historic preservation. But neither can our opponents. Not conclusively, nor even approximately, given the rigidity of opinions on both sides. And certainly not in time for the districting vote.

And yet the vote still comes. It comes because the Supreme Court has said that historic districting is constitutional, whatever property rightists may say.

Even if property rightists can't win the constitutional battle in Washington, their local followers here can use the seed of their ideas to sow discord and doubt in our local designation process. All they have to do, remember, is to keep us from making our case and winning Council approval. We in turn want to push them to ridiculous extremes.

MYTH AND COMMON SENSE

The basic libertarian message is plain. The political task of the good citizen, it claims, is to defend freedom against a long rising tide of reliance upon government that has steadily eroded the legacy of liberty bequeathed to us by the Founding Fathers.

When it comes to property rights, this is a call to duty without sacrifice. It's easy to live up to a principle that says you may do with your property as you please. It's also pleasing to be told that you're affirming a precept hard-won by American patriots when you do whatever you want with your property.

This is political mythmaking of a very high order. It hijacks American history to deal with today's complicated property issues in seductively simplistic terms.

We, on our side, have nothing quite so ingratiating. Our advantage in the rights skirmish lies in the common sense of our less ideological, more hospitable neighbors who are still undecided.

Those takers know from their own practical lives that citizens have both individual rights and public responsibilities. They prize freedom, and still they know that good government is the handmaiden, not the enemy of the people.

I say they *know* this at some level because they live it daily. We all do. Responsible liberty, the rule of law, the gift of representative government—all are threads in the golden skein of citizenship that runs the long length of our political culture.

Ask Americans what they value most and they'll say freedom. We all like small government in principle, but in practice we expect more from government than to just leave us alone. We want leaders and laws that reflect our values and protect our property against the whims of others who care less—and are careless—about us. We also want a government that knows and values the communities where we live, just like we want to live and work with people who know how to be good neighbors.

So we don't have to lecture takers as if we were insisting on something new. We can identify ourselves with what they already know as true simply by reminding them of it.

We don't have to worry about proving our opponents wrong, either, because they're not self-evidently right. The best they can do is reimagine the past in their own idealized image of the way we were once—and how we ought to be again. But that's not the way we really were then, and it surely isn't the world of our experience today.

THE POVERTY OF LIBERTARIANISM

That's why libertarianism is an ideology and radical property rightists are ideological extremists. Don't forget it.

An ideology is a political philosophy that claims we can have the life we deserve if we leave hold of the one we're in. Ideologies can be left wing or right wing—or simply, as some libertarians describe themselves, antiauthority. But they are always radical because they reject the normal way we commonly think and commonly are.

Always radical, as I say, yet never more so than in the hand-to-hand combat of local politics. Here followers tend to select from a credo whatever they please, jettison nuance, and express themselves in absolutes.

"Historic preservation," a radical breaker insists, "does not involve conflicts between property 'rights' and 'responsibilities.' There is never such a conflict. People have property rights and everyone's responsibility is not to violate those rights."[2]

But just saying it doesn't make it so. What's more, the courts have repeatedly said it isn't so.

That's why radical property rightists like to appeal for relief to the higher court of history and the political philosophies of the Founders. But, in truth, those who embrace an all-or-nothing notion of private property rights are willful historical amnesiacs with an impoverished sense of history.

HIJACKING HISTORY

Government has regulated private property in America for more than 300 years. All colonized land began as Crown property that was parceled out to individuals and groups who found favor. No explorer ever splashed ashore claiming land "for me, Freddie Crumpton of Parsley Lane, Upper Whampton, Cheshire." There never was a time in which a right to any land in the American colonies stood in opposition to the interests of the state as a general precept.

Later, the Revolution didn't change things much, either. The legal traditions that the framers took with them into the Constitutional Convention in Philadelphia were extensions of, not breaks with, deeply rooted English practices.

So what is the true genius of our form of governance? Well, it's not a rawboned liberty to do as we please. It's our concept of *free-*

dom under law. In our tradition, there is nothing of the freedom of the fox in the henhouse!

Jefferson's "inalienable rights" and the Bill of Rights with its Fifth Amendment property protections were advanced to shield us from capricious governmental power. But they were never meant to absolve us from political and legal responsibility to each other for the public good—the commonweal—or else the rest of the Declaration of Independence and the Constitution are nonsense.

The foundation of American liberty is the belief that people *when they are free* also choose wisely and well when what they do affects others—like exercising property rights. But this country wasn't founded on just crossed fingers, hoping for the best. The drafters of the Constitution knew the all too human tendency to choose badly at the expense of others. So they empowered us to make laws to guide and inform decision making *and* to restrain us when we cross the line by failing to exercise good judgment.

We were meant to be a self-governed people, not an ungoverned one, even when it came to property. No one has a right to wreck a neighbor's setting, a block, or a neighborhood. Our profound attachment to liberty assumes we all understand this. Laws are rightfully made for those who don't. Those willful few who feel the pinch of law may yelp "freedom!" but it's the rule of law that protects the freedom of the rest from the irresponsible actions of the few.

Those who wish us no good are often the loudest, most insistent defenders of a nonexistent freedom to do with their property as they choose. What they say should be an affront to average law-abiding citizens who know and care about their friends and neighbors.

So let's give our radical breakers no comfort. Let's not dignify their assertions with debate. We have one sharp point to make: *the enemy of liberty is not law or government but the argument that people are by right uncontrollable.*

Our adversaries may hijack history. They just can't make it take them where they want to go.

THE WEALTH OF NATIONS

But can they buy their way out of restraints? "It boils down to your right as an American to do what you want to with what you pay for," says an opponent.[3]

Oh, my. Let's see now. Money changing hands confers an absolute right? Pure piffle!

Still, there's the more sophisticated dodge that some find in the free market economic theories first propounded by Adam Smith in *The Wealth of Nations* (1776). His basic assumption was that buyers and sellers, by freely exchanging goods at negotiated prices in an unfettered marketplace, not only were able to satisfy themselves but also advance the welfare of all.

He explained this in a now famous passage: a man (as he put it) while pursuing his own self-interest, "is in, as in many other cases, led by an *invisible hand* to promote an end which was no part of his intention." As David Ricardo summed it up, "the pursuit of individual advantage is admirably connected with the universal good of the whole."

Radical property rightists love this stuff! It lets them replace political law with economic laws—those impersonal economic forces that have no responsibility to any of us, no conscience and no need to worry about outcomes. Just get yourself down to Market Street at the intersection of supply and demand where free competition allocates resources among competing self-interests. Whatever happens there is said to be as good as it gets.

THE COLLAPSE OF IDEOLOGY

And what does this mean for preservation? "The free market will determine which property is worth preserving—and which is not," says Dimitri Vassilaros, Pittsburgh columnist and talk radio's "The

Lovable Libertarian," who advises other libertarians not to "be quick to handcuff the invisible hand and replace it with heavy-handed government."[4]

But what if the invisible hand becomes the fickle finger of fate? Free marketeers can be blasé about how the self-correcting market will punish mistakes . . . until someone does something unsightly next door to them! Think globally, grouse locally, huh?

Vassilaros himself sees the problem. The solution? "As with any homeowner association, the owners of properties in historic districts could draft rules and regulations for themselves, if there were truly support for such an association."

Is that so? Then why not use government? I suppose—I haven't heard him say—it's because our democracy allows the majority to conclude for a dissenting minority. That would be—what?—coercive, I suppose, to brother libertarians.

Plato had their number long ago. We're told in *The Republic* of those ungovernable sons who've moved past liberty to license, who acknowledge no law, doing as they please and pleasing no one but themselves. This, he said, is democracy run amuck.

THE SKINNY ON RADICALS

A community meeting, of course, isn't a political theory seminar. When hard-wired property rightists trot out their authorities, tell them that if you shared their views you'd try to dress them up too.

I want you to think of their ideological garb as the emperor's new clothes. Once you see through it you'll find that *the fiercest property rightists are indistinguishable from those strong-willed and self-absorbed opponents who, true to type in every community, simply don't like being told what to do.*

That's the naked truth of it. Make sure that the rest of the crowd sees it, too. It will make a lasting impression.

WHAT TO DO

So where does that leave us? For all practical purposes, we've stopped their momentum. Now we can think about how to get rid of them. Here's how it might work for you:

When you've made your pitch for designation and breakers start in with their challenges, listen very carefully to see where they're headed.

- If you get garden-variety questions—like, *Why would anyone want to create another layer of government?*—then respond as in the last two chapters.
- But if they turn out to be of the ideological hothouse variety—such as, *Real preservationists should preserve our tradition of liberty!*—then you might want to turn tables on them and put them on the Q&A spot.

Invite them to stand and explain themselves. Ask questions *as if* you really *are* confused. "Are you telling us that historic districts are illegal?" "Then how is it that there are 2,000 districts in the country?" "Does the Supreme Court agree with your position?"

These questions will seem perfectly reasonable to everyone but your opponents. They can't afford to answer them factually. So they'll likely turn to ideology and fabricated history. Once they start down that road, you're the one who's going to sound like the voice of common sense.

Make the subtext of the exchange "Whom do you trust?" and act so that your neighbors are more comfortable with you than with your adversaries. Through it all, be friendly, solicitous, attentive, unflappable, unimpressed, and confident.

Reach out to takers who are wavering. Empathize with them over their decision. Tell them you believe in property rights, too, *and* that you believe in family-friendly community values and good government. Remind them that real choices are never black-and-white.

Stress that districting is just a *practical* arrangement, no more or less extensive than the job that needs to be done. That's all. Just practical people taking care of practical business.

Say again that historic districts have passed constitutional muster. Wonder aloud how some would push their own extreme notions of property rights while denying us our *political right* to do what the Supreme Court has said is legitimate.

Sooner or later the radical property rightists will insist—as they *always* do—that their objection to districting is a matter of principle. "It comes down to personal philosophy and the role of government," an architect and property rights association member says.[5]

Thoughtfully agree that you're sure that it is . . . *for them*. Make it clear, however, that *for you*, where you stand, it's about *people*, your neighbors, their real-world issues—what they care about, what they hope for—and *practical* results for them and their families.

Say, "Thank you so much for telling us what we *can't* do, in your opinion. But we've got real-life issues here that need positive *can-do* thinking and effective community action."

That's your wedge issue. Place it firmly between the takers and breakers. Then drive home the point. Insist that there's enough goodwill in the audience to make a district *possible*, and regrettably enough . . . well, enough of the opposite . . . to make it *necessary*. If your strike rings true, community opinion should split your way.

The one sure thing is that your opponents won't look as good as they did when they walked through the door. But keep in mind that it won't mean a thing if it doesn't put signatures on our petition.

NOTES

1. "Protecting Private Property Rights from Regulatory Takings. Testimony of Roger Pilon," *CATO Congressional Testimony*, February 10, 1995, www.cato.org/testimony.

2. Rex Curry, rexy.net, n.d.

3. Kevin Duffy, "History a Matter of Heart in Newnan," www.ajc.com, *Atlanta Constitution-Journal*, June 9, 2003.

4. "Point/Counterpoint," *Libertarian Forum*, vol. 3, no. 6, September, 1996.

5. John Dicker, "Preservation or Coercion? Manitou's Historic District Polarizes Property Owners," www.csindy.com, i-News, October 3–9, 2002.

TWENTY-THREE

Petition Politics

How do I love thee? Let me count the ways.

—Elizabeth Barrett Browning

Like love, historic districting sooner or later gets down to number crunching. But what numbers, and what ways? Property owner support, mainly. And by petition, mandated or not.

WHO GETS POLLED?

We want a clean, persuasive petition. That means property owners only. No renters, no leaseholders, no live-in relatives, no store managers, no employees, no friends, no named heirs. Nothing but property owners, period, unless the City directs us otherwise.

Our opponents might not be so careful. Comparing our petitions, then, will be like comparing apples and oranges. Our petition should be like a polished apple and poison to their effort.

What about polling others, too? Suppose we want to revitalize a shopping district. Then let's survey business owners with a *separate*, rigorously defined petition.

DRAFTING YOUR PETITION

Draft your petition defensively. Imagine how your opponents might attack it.

1. Top of the page: What are you asking people to agree to? Be sure the petition says what you want it to say so there can be no misunderstanding. Brevity is good, but clarity is better. Don't just write a heading that says "We support the Historic District." That's vague and arguably misleading:

- It doesn't identify who "we" are and why "we" have a stake in the district.
- It doesn't define what "support" means.
- It doesn't clearly convey that signers know what they're supporting.

While you consider that for a moment, let's look at how we'll handle signatures.

2. Constructing the list of owners: When was the last time you signed a petition? Did someone outside the grocery store hand you a clipboard with some statement at the top? Were you asked to sign on the next line?

Well, we can't afford to be that informal and disorganized. Circulating a petition might *seem* that simple at first. But what will you do when you've collected a number of signatures and questions start popping up?

Like what? Suppose Tom Brown all by himself owns three parcels of land in the district: a Victorian home, a vacant lot, and an apartment building. What property is he thinking about when he signs? All of them? What if he later says he was thinking about buildings, not the lot?

Now suppose Mary and Bob Smith live in an older home—one parcel. He signs the petition, and later she signs on another sheet. Do they count twice as much as Tom? How do you know they own the same property instead of two or more, or whether they own them jointly or separately?

See what I mean? Our opponents will see it, and they'll say our petition can't be trusted. Any lack of clarity and rigor in our methodology is an invitation to trouble.

The solution is to list every property in the district by its official parcel number. *Each* and *every* owner of record for each individual property should be listed and given a separate line for signing *no matter how many times they have to sign*. Their mailing addresses should be listed with their names, along with telephone numbers for verifying signatures.

Page 174 shows a sample petition page that gets the heading and listing right and is easy to use. Repeat the declaration at the top of every page, or signers may claim they didn't see it. Now look at it.

Who *are* Tom Brown and Mary and Bob Smith that they should appear at the start of our petition? That's not a very democratic question but it's an important political one.

When you hand folks a clipboard, you want them to see right away that they'll be joining a prestigious and growing group. Let's say you've got fifteen parcels listed on the first two pages. Make sure they're owned by well-known and respected supporters from every major constituency group in the district.

Get *all* of them to sign before you go to the wider public. Eyes will be drawn to any gap in signatures. "Why the dissent?" folks will wonder. A solid phalanx of signatures says that the district is a good idea and well on its way to success. As Donald Trump says, people want to be seen with winners.

PROPOSED [NAME] HISTORIC DISTRICT PETITION

We, the undersigned owners of properties contained within the boundaries of the proposed Historic District, do hereby request that our property be included in the district, to be administered under the City zoning
ordinance [number]. I have been informed about historic district designation and understand how it will affect my property.

PROPERTY OWNERS IN FAVOR OF
ESTABLISHING THE LOCAL HISTORIC DISTRICT

Name/Address	Parcel No.	Signature(s)	Date
1. ROBERT SMITH MARY SMITH 26 Market Street City, State, Zip Code (555) 213-4567	1606-273-1	_____	____
2. THOMAS BROWN 564 Hill Lane City, State, Zip Code (555) 213-8901	1606-273-36	_____	____
3. THOMAS BROWN 564 Hill Lane City, State, Zip Code (555) 213-8901	1606-273-47	_____	____

But then how do you list the rest of the property owners? Al-
phabetically or by street address, for signing convenience. No one
is going to care that the initial dozen or so names are out of order.

3. Unilateral exclusions: There are sound political reasons for
leaving some owners alone. Say there's a private swim club that
owns its property. It has members for and against designation. Do

---

PARCELS EXCLUDED AS COMMUNITY-WIDE INSTITUTIONS

178. SWIM CLUB   1606-273-89   <u>EXCLUDED</u>   _____
      20 H Street
      City, State, Zip Code
      (555) 213-3334

---

you ask for the club's support and open an internal debate? How about the local church?

You might want to hold off even if you're fairly certain of their support. Don't give your opponents another reason for saying that you're dividing the community—only this time you're pitting club members—no, worse: church members—against each other! Folks you're trying to win over won't like having their place of play or worship politicized. This goes for the local school, too, in most cases.

Unilaterally declare these places out of bounds. Just say you'd rather give their votes to the opposition than to embroil them in controversy. This alone is proof that you're not maliciously dividing the community.

List these excluded parcels at the end. Put them under a general heading such as shown in the sample above.

Notify each excluded property owner of record. Be sure to include a justification. Then explain your rationale in the petition summary you'll be sending to the City Council.

SECURING SIGNATURES

There's a double meaning here: collecting signatures and keeping the originals safe.

Give copies of the petition to trusted canvassers. Make sure they know not to let anyone sign for anyone else—even a spouse—unless there is good reason, and then *record that reason*.

Remind them that "leaning" counts only in horseshoes and Pisa. We can't go to the Planning Commission, for instance, and say we have 38 percent for the district and 15 percent leaning toward us. That'll only draw attention to why some are hesitating.

What do we do if there are property owners who live at a distance? We talk to them by phone and then send them copies of their signature pages to return by mail or fax.

Retain every page having an original signature on it. In the end you might have scores—in large districts, a hundred or so—of original signature sheets to submit as part of the formal record. Photocopy them and then use those copies to cut and paste together a master petition.

Put information on your website telling folks where they may sign a petition. When they do sign, try to get their e-mail addresses so you can keep them updated online.

Note: Cyber petitions—where signing is done online—is a recent and not yet generally accepted substitute for hardcopy signatures. So be careful if you're thinking that way.

DECLARATIONS OF NEUTRALITY

There's always the chance you'll run into a few folks who don't want to take sides. They're like the old Southern politician who, when asked where he stood on an issue, said, "Wa'll, some of mah friends are fer it and some of mah friends are agin' it, and Ah'm fer mah friends."

If you can't persuade them to sign in favor of designation and they say they won't sign against it, then get them to sign on the line as neutral. That way, if they show up on your opponents' side you can call a foul on ya'll's friend.

AN OFFICIAL MAIL-IN SURVEY

It's not unusual for the authorities to direct planning staff to conduct a poll by mail-in postcard or consent form. Don't let this probe be a substitute for your own effort. The reasons are obvious:

1. We don't know if the database they'll use is complete and accurate.
2. We can't be assured they'll use the right survey methodology.
3. No one will be as diligent as we in addressing, sending out, receiving, securing, and collating the postcards and then compiling an accurate and usable list.
4. Mailed surveys are notoriously unreliable indicators of opinion since they also reflect such bad habits as not reading mail and procrastinating.
5. They don't afford us an opportunity to state our case as we request a signature.
6. We might not have access to the results to check them and draw conclusions.

If the City goes ahead with a mailing after you've voiced reservations, then respectfully tell everyone that you have more confidence in your own petition. If their findings differ from yours, challenge those findings.

SUBMITTING THE PETITION

When should you submit the petition? It depends on your jurisdiction. A very few cities require a majority just to get the proposal on the HPC's agenda. Most don't require a petition at all. Usual practice has the petition filed just prior to the City Council meeting. Just don't wait to make it public at the hearing. It won't be credible because it can't be verified.

So check with City Hall. But when filing time comes, make last-minute amendments for any intervening deaths, divorces, property transfers, or changes in the proposed district's physical borders. Add optional surveys and testimonials. Send copies to the Mayor and each commission or City Council member, and get another copy to the Planning Department.

But first attach a cover letter explaining in executive summary—one page only—your method for counting and weighing support. Then tell them what all these signatures add up to.

COUNTING AND WEIGHING SUPPORT

"How do I count thee?" Ms. Browning might write as a petition manager. "Let me love the ways."

You mean there's more than one? Sure. Let me give you an example using this data:

Table 23.1

	For		Against	
J. Stringfellow	4 parcels (.5 acres each)		G. Farmer M. Farmer R. Farmer A. Farmer	1 parcel (2 acres)

How do we count them? One in favor of designation and four opposed? Or is it four in favor and one opposed? Obviously that depends on whether we're counting people or parcels. Here's why:

1. **Counting people:** In favor of counting people is the basic idea of "one person, one vote." In fact, we're usually asked, "How many people support your proposal?" Yet not all folks own equal shares.

   So we have another choice: Do we count each name equally? Or do we count multiple owners of a parcel fractionally? If we don't count them fractionally, then how do we deal with jointly owning couples who differ on districting?

2. **Counting parcels:** In favor of parcels is the fact that we're designating properties, not owners. But why do we assume all parcels are created equal? Let me cite two examples of where this question has been critical:

- In Newton, Massachusetts, in 2002, a historic district was being resisted by Lasell College, which owned *two-thirds* of the property in the district.
- In 2004, Virginia considered adding 172 private parcels to the historic district covering the Manassas National Battlefield Park. Each parcel was assigned one vote, regardless of size or number of owners. A county supervisor called that unfair, since a large farm could be forced into the district by a few small landholders.

And, while we're letting our minds run down this road, what would happen if someone—an opponent, say—were to subdivide a single large tract in the midst of our campaign?

3. **Counting acreage:** So should we be calculating acreage and assigning proportional weight accordingly? It's hard to do, but it can be done. The acreage estimates in our sample slice are a total wash, two acres for and two acres against.

But before we start counting acreage across the whole petition—or for that matter, before we decide to count either people or parcels—what do we want to know?

You and I need to know which method—counting acreage *or* people *or* parcels—is going to give us the best statistical showing to support districting. So get the petition finished first. Then we'll decide how to count the fors and againsts.

There's a word for this kind of statistical analysis: *politics.*

CHAPTER TWENTY-THREE

AN OFFICIAL COUNTING METHOD

So now don't tell me you're going to ask the City Council who or what and how they'd like you to count, unless you already know that there is an officially established way of doing it. You'll just confuse them. Or if you're really unlucky maybe someone there who sees the issue will stack the methodology against us.

We'd better keep the decision in our own hands if we can. As long as the City keeps silent, any method we choose is as legitimate as any other. Conversely, of course, they're all equally fudgy.

THE MAGIC NUMBER

Has your City Council targeted a minimum support level for designation? Most don't. New Orleans is an example. Others, like Block Island, Illinois, specify 51 percent. Baltimore wants to see a "healthy" majority. Traverse City, Michigan, and Valparaiso, Illinois, require at least a two-thirds majority.

Targets can be very unfair. And, no, I don't mean because they're arbitrary or because preservation is too important to be left to majorities.

The problem is whether the target is, say, 51 percent of all property owners—regardless of how we count them—or 51 percent of all property owners *signing petitions*. The problem is the same with a postcard mail-in. Is the City looking for 51 percent support among all cards *sent out* or all cards *returned*?

Besides, who's going to do the deciding? Let's say the Director of Planning tells us to count people and just make sure we have more signers than our opponents do. Is this the HPC's and the Planning Commission's position, too, and shared by every member? How about the Mayor and City Council? Unless criteria are established by ordinance, you have to assume they'll shift on you or simply be ignored.

There's a word for that, too. Guess what. And politics means that you've got to be prepared for everything.

If you can't reach a majority target of *all* property owners because some folks either don't respond or won't sign their name to anything, then keep a list of them. If you do achieve the minimum goal, don't stop working. Nothing is ever certain or final in politics.

Even if the City Council has specified the counting method and target, use other methods that'll show you in a more favorable light. They're politicians after all. Their careers are built on slicing and dicing numbers.

In the end, the magic number you have to reach is *any* number that they'll start quoting in your favor.

TWENTY-FOUR

Reaching Out to the Opposition

There's only you and me and we just disagree.

—Jim Krueger, "We Just Disagree"

It's very difficult to lead, to project a practical vision for our community, to take flak, and then to go talk with folks who may have publicly reviled us. Still, we have to do it and *be seen doing it*.

We're not ethically responsible for this fight, so no apologies. That's the kind of self-inflicted guilt that victim mongers trade in.

Let's keep our political priorities straight. We're not out to prove we're the good guys and opponents are the bad guys. It's enough that we disagree.

Our aim is district designation. Our opponent's aim is to deny us. Neither of us has a primary interest in making peace.

Yet ill will can be a problem for us if decision makers down at City Hall see us as unwilling to meet and talk with the other side. From this angle, outreach is damage control.

That's for appearance's sake. Yet there are substantive advantages as well. Small compromises now can save big compromises later. And talks may help us whittle down our opposition.

A CALIBRATED DIPLOMACY

Up to now I've treated breakers as a singular group of adversaries. We've even lumped curmudgeons and ideologues together in order to push undecided takers toward us to get us to the vital political center.

Yet the opposition is neither monolithic nor static. We have a vision and they have objections, and those objections to our plan will vary from person to person and over time.

So we need a nuanced, calibrated approach. Direct talks can help us better understand what each property owner wants. We may also be able to correct misperceptions, establish a measure of trust, make targeted offers, and split some opponents off from the die hards.

As for the rest—especially property rights extremists—we simply have differing worldviews. We argue it round and they argue it flat. The best we can do is agree to disagree. But it's never really that nice.

NEGOTIATING

Outreach entails the possibility of compromise, and that means you have to think like a negotiator. The skills you'll need are more akin to those of a manager, composing differences to move forward, than those of a visionary leader setting the mark.

There are plenty of books out there on the art of negotiation. They tell you about styles—competitive versus collaborative, combative versus passive, good cop and bad cop, dos and don'ts, and even how to control your body language.

But never mind all that. Ours is a one-shot deal, not a career. At our neighborhood level, it's most important just to talk and listen. Still it helps to bear in mind three hard-and-fast rules:

1. Never negotiate out of weakness.
2. Never compromise vital interests.
3. Be prepared.

Keep notes on specific points opponents make. Talk within your steering committee about where concessions might be made and then prioritize them. Work out fallback positions. Be clear about what is to be negotiated. Define the issues, get the facts. Think in terms of ambiguity to paper over differences. And make sure everybody on our side is onboard before sealing a deal.

THREE VENUES

There are three types of face-to-face meetings:

1. **Individual:** Individual one-on-one talks are the best way to deal with minor opponents—those who aren't leading the resistance and have their own issues. In every community there are a few folks who dig in their heels but don't want to be associated with loudmouthed and abusive resisters. We can respect their differences and still help them to a kind of useful neutrality.
2. **Group:** Meet with any self-identified group of opponents that is the rough equivalent of our steering committee. Both sides should be comfortable with the setting. Insist on knowing exactly for whom the other party speaks and whether

they have authority to conclude agreements on behalf of ab-
sentees.

3. **Community:** A community-wide meeting moderated by a
mutually acceptable facilitator has several advantages. No
opponent can later claim to have been excluded or denied a
voice in community forums. Politicians in particular will see
it as an unforced and highly desirable contribution to due
process.

Be careful, though. Do not accept *arbitration*, which means a
binding settlement or judgment by an independent third party.
We're talking about *mediation* here, where the facilitator more simply helps the sides talk about what's important and keep them on
track.

Screen proposed moderators carefully. Some of these folks see
themselves as professional peacemakers. They want community
without conflict, and they may think that the goal of all politics is
consensus at any price—even at the frustration of good public
policy.

The last thing we want is for a mediator to start finger-pointing,
because sure as shootin', as long as we're the stronger party, we will
be the target. But a final report by an independent mediator that at-
tests to a good faith—yet inconclusive—effort to compose differences can clear up doubts and open the way to a decisive Council
vote.

KEEP RECORDS

Keep track of all letters, phone calls, and meetings with opponents.
Note who was contacted, what was discussed, when it occurred,
and where it took place. Write out what our side offered and what
responses we got.

Be careful about what you say. Put offers of concessions in writing and always frame them in terms of strengths not weaknesses. Never, ever, put in writing that you find value in their position, sympathize with their concerns, or feel their pain. They will turn it against you.

Get all agreements in writing and signed by all participants. Consider them insurance policies against later misunderstanding.

PROTECT YOUR BASE

As you continue to talk with opponents, don't take your supporters for granted. Don't water down the district to the point where it becomes:

- inconsequential.
- a burden on property owners without real benefit.
- a benefit to property owners without serving preservation interests.

The more things you concede the greater will be the potential threat to your leadership. On the other hand, solid progress can come as a relief to anyone who has reluctantly stood with us.

So keep your base well-informed. There might not be any truly bad guys around, but there are good guys for certain. We need to be most careful of their interests and keep them close.

TWENTY-FIVE

Moving on to City Hall

Our similarities are different.

—Dale Berra on his father, Yogi

We've done it all.

We've learned to think politically about preservation and to strategize. We've looked around our neighborhood, read the lay of the political landscape, and crafted a practical vision. We've gained confidence and public support in community meetings. We have brought forth a newly vital sense of community in the midst of continuing conflict over districting.

Now we've got to do it all again, but differently.

It's time for us to take our show on the road. We're going to translate our community successes into votes for designation in public hearings before the HPC and the Planning Commission as we move toward final City Council approval.

Prepare to shift gears. We'll be dealing with people who have interests and responsibilities different from those we've encountered in our community meetings. The public hearing format will be different, too.

DUE PROCESS

We will no longer be in charge of setting the meeting agenda and managing debate. In fact, there will probably be no interplay at all between those for and against districting—just separate presentations from the floor.

That's because we're getting procedural due process, and nothing more. Due process is our constitutional right to be notified of an impending action and be heard on it. But once the meeting is gaveled to order the give-and-take between citizens and public officials is mainly a one-way street. We *give* testimony and they *take* it. What they do with it is up to them.

So what will we say to them and how will we say it? We don't want to be like the cuckoo in Shakespeare's *Henry IV*, "Heard, not regarded."

Do we tell them why we want a historic district? Yes, by all means. And our opponents will say they don't want it. So how will decision makers decide the issue?

The answer depends on what commissioners bring with them to the hearings. So it's a good idea to do whatever we can *now* to influence their preparation. If you agree with me—and I'm sure you do—then we ought to think about a strategy for working with the planners who act as HPC and Planning Commission staff.

ACTING THE LEADER

You have taken a leadership role, literally. You've seized it by your own actions.

Do you remember that first time we walked into the Planning Department to ask about districting? We represented only ourselves and a few others then.

Things have changed. Now you speak for a large portion of our community. You've attained the stature of a recognized leader. You've kept planners informed of your progress. They've been invited to attend our local meetings. They've watched you gain popular support for designation. Your success should make you their dependable partner.

So what does it get us? Can we parlay our status into an advantage?

That is a delicate question. Planning staff will be—as they *should* be—protective of their prerogatives and responsibilities. We don't want to compromise their standing with decision makers. And we certainly have no interest in jeopardizing their willingness to work with us.

But by now they also have a professional stake in our success. They've been working on the official side of the designation process. They've put together the districting proposal, shepherded the study through SHPO, and worked on the text of the legislation to be approved. They have coordinated the Planning Department's effort and probably brought it to the attention of the City Manager and other administrators.

It's in our interests to work collaboratively together from here on out. Yet we want to avoid the appearance of improper collusion. What we ask of staff has to be within the scope of their legitimate functions. Our main interest is seeing that commissioners are well informed about the district proposal and their role in recommending it to the Council.

We also need to guard against procedural glitches or irregularities. If you live in a town where overworked staff could use some help, you might act as de facto project manager, keeping track of everything that has to be done, by whom and when. But no matter where you are, I suggest you get staff to help you put together two "maps" for your own benefit:

1. An organizational chart of every City office—with personnel appended—that will be involved in designation.
2. A flowchart of the approval process down to the last detail of who signs off on what and when, with drop-dead dates for submissions highlighted.

The simple act of putting them together can be a useful exercise even for planning staff who have done it all before.

Check from time to time to see that everyone is on track, signing off on every detail, scheduling every meeting, meeting every deadline. Do it with a light touch, though. Treat everyone with courtesy and respect. Make regular friendly visits to the Planning Department.

Offer assistance. Many departments don't have a preservationist on staff. Your own specialist might contribute to the background information packets that should go to commissioners. But make certain that there's a firewall up between what is done for you and for the City, one that can sustain reasonable scrutiny about a conflict of interests.

DEVELOPING BRIEFING PACKETS

While I'm on the subject, we should be preparing to send our own information to commissioners. But there is a difference between what we mail out and what staff provides.

The Planning Department's packets should contain *documents* and *factual materials*: copies of the draft legislation, the district map and survey study summary, the criteria by which the district was drawn, perhaps a compilation of relevant court decisions, and any number of brief statements on such technical matters as what a zoning overlay district means and how design guidelines function.

Whatever isn't covered by the Planning Department will have to be added to our own packets. Avoid overlap and anything at variance with their information.

If you're able to contribute, do what you can to make their information packet *brief* to invite reading and *comprehensive* so it's sufficient. Be deliberative. Don't just think "guidelines!" and toss some photocopied pamphlet into the mix. Find the best source. Edit or summarize it. Don't expect commissioners to wade through more than what is absolutely on point. They'll just lay it aside.

Our own packets should make our *political points* in a brief and commonsensical format. But how can we know which points to hit?

PROFILING COMMISSIONERS

We'll first need to know everything political about anyone who is going to weigh in on designation. If you haven't found a political insider as I suggested in chapter 8, then you'll have to do your own spadework.

Start with the HPC. Ask staff about the chair and other commissioners. They may be reticent until you explain that you're not asking them to reveal confidential information.

- How do they see the commission functioning in public session?
- Who takes the lead in discussions?
- Are there policy or personality cliques?
- Who tends to agree with whom?
- Are there any outstanding issues that regularly arise—say, of a budgetary, personnel, or program priority nature—that can affect our interests?

Next, cross-reference what you've heard with a former commissioner or two if you can. A local preservation organization that's
taken an active role in commission proceedings can be a good
source of independent insights. The same thing goes for architects
or contractors who've made regular appearances.

Analyze HPC minutes for the last year or so. Check your local
newspaper archive for informative stories. While you're at it, pay attention to bylines. We're going to be looking for a reporter in chapter 27.

Put together a political profile of each member and double
check their terms of office. Someone might cycle off the HPC before you get there.

Now do the same thing all over again for the Planning Commission.

Once you've researched the book on them, go see the movie.
Attend as many HPC and Planning Commission meetings as you
can squeeze in. You might not learn much new, but you'll start getting comfortable with the setup.

And keep your mouth shut! Resist speaking out. Your dog is in
nobody's fight but ours.

Now that we've established our presence in City Hall and gath-
ered passive intelligence, we're ready to move over to a more active
role. Next we'll be working behind the scenes to develop the information we need for plotting the next stages.

TWENTY-SIX

Behind-the-Scenes Intelligence

All rising to a great place is by a winding stair.

—Francis Bacon

Now to the obvious question: Why don't we just talk with each commissioner face-to-face?

Your local jurisdiction might not permit direct, so-called *ex parte*, contacts outside of advertised meetings. Normally, that's the case when commissions are acting on permit applications.

But our situation is different, isn't it? The district proposal also isn't ours, technically. The Planning Department is bringing the proposal forward, albeit on our initiative. We are supporting new legislation, not asking if a project conforms to existing laws.

So get a ruling from the City Attorney or your local ethics commission. Make sure everyone knows the answer. We want our opponents playing by the same rules, and no misinformed accusations flying about.

If you can meet one-on-one, show them what you're made of. A private meeting is in a class of its own when it comes to taking another person's measure—theirs and *yours*.

Don't go in expecting straight talk. You might get it, but private citizens serving on commissions tend to be less open than elected officials who are used to talking about legislation. To discover what they're really thinking, we want to draw them out with their guard down. Just like in chess, we'll try to catch them looking the other way.

A PROCEDURAL GAMBIT

Anecdotal evidence—but a ton of it—suggests it's the rare member of any commission who has ever read through its enabling ordinance and rules of procedure. But *you* ought to read them. Then open your gambit by asking planning staff to explain to you specifically how the commissions will function in the designation process.

That innocent question might get you a blank stare. Why? Because our kind of hearing is unusual in most localities, and even staff might not have thought about it much.

Appointed commissions mainly *interpret and apply existing ordinances* to applications that come before them. Most have little experience in *advising on making laws*, and practically no institutional memory from case to case apart from long-serving staff. Each sitting board tends to make up its own interpretation on the fly—and does so for better or worse.

Commissioners just can't seem to resist acting like policy makers, not advisors. Instead of passing on how the district will affect preservation and planning, they'll presume to decide what's good for the community by their own lights. Take this, for example, from a Planning Board chair talking about the opposition:

I don't blame them. I wouldn't want my house in a historic district either. It's another layer of bureaucracy. I'm not dead set against it. But the more I think about it the more I am. It's ridiculous to have to get a permit to [replace] porch flooring. . . . Just think if they had that mentality of not wanting change back when they started putting bathrooms inside houses. If you wanted to keep everything like it is, we'd still be using outhouses.

This is risky business, from our perspective.

Never mind his house isn't in our neighborhood; that even as a commissioner he's unwilling to consider community interests beyond his front porch; that there isn't the slightest inkling here of an understanding of what it means to be a neighbor; and that he hasn't been present at the meetings where we've convinced many of our neighbors differently. It's enough that he seems to think he is allowed to step into the shoes of an anonymous homeowner in the district and, unlike the rest of us, be able to vote a commission position—and vote his prejudices.

So our next move is to ask staff to give each commission an up-to-date briefing on its *advisory role* in the process, detailing the scope of what they're to cover and what the City Council is looking for in their recommendations.

How the briefing takes place is unimportant. It might be at an administrative meeting or special workshop. Leave it up to them. As a Chinese leader once said, it doesn't matter what color the cat is as long as it catches mice.

Just don't settle for a briefing by memo. If you encounter resistance, point out that it'll also be an excellent opportunity to walk commissioners through the documentary and technical materials they'll be receiving.

In fact, insist upon it. This will test your relationship with staff. But if there is ever a place to test it, *this is it.*

Experienced staff are well aware of how routinely commissioners come to meetings well intentioned yet less than adequately prepared—and then turn around and blame staff for their own mistakes. Staff should jump at the chance to cover their bases.

Besides, we have a right to a fair and proper hearing. Testifying before ill-informed commissioners is like striking matches on soap.

AN UNGUARDED WINDOW

Our angle is simple. Any effort to set commissioners straight should get them to reveal their current thinking.

How? Staff have to prepare for the briefing. Don't you think they'd benefit from getting each commissioner to send in questions or comments in advance? Nothing particularly well-informed, you know, just whatever comes to mind.

And why not? It makes staff look solicitous and responsive. It's protection, too. They can't very well be blamed for giving the commission what it requests. It will also insure them against surprise questions in public, especially ones that put them in a bad light.

These submissions will be as unguarded a window as we're likely to get into commissioners' attitudes toward districting. And that, my friend, is invaluable intelligence.

Whatever they submit will be a matter of public record. If staff is uncomfortable sharing it, then suggest they compile the responses in a memorandum for the commission and make it available for public review. Still, do your best to find out *who* is asking *what* questions.

I have one such memo from a planning commissioner. In summary, he asked:

1. Has the process been tainted and biased by proponents and planning staffers?

2. Has the public been provided copies of all relevant statutes and policies?
3. Can individual owners ask to be excluded under existing state and local law?
4. What criteria determine historic significance?
5. Who determines the boundaries and by what authority is that power exercised?
6. Have any proponents or staff made incorrect or misleading statements?
7. Has the planning staff been fair and evenhanded in dealing with all parties?
8. Why haven't proponents been willing to compromise?
9. Is any other self-appointed group studying other districts without public knowledge?

The background check showed him to be a real estate broker and property rights advocate who *always* voted against regulation. Those questions—mostly accusations, some offensive—could smother us if we met up with them at the hearing for the first time. I think staff would feel the same way, don't you?

A swing voter on the same commission summed up his central concern: "Can we encourage designs that have historic significance and not unrealistically burden the property owner?" Still another said the majority was taking advantage of the minority and wanted a compromise. A third could find no justification for excluding opposition owners, while a fourth was uneasy about designating property over owners' objections. Coming out of the same meeting, the chair concluded that key issues for most members were:

1. Whether a historic district is a public taking of private property.
2. The "another layer of bureaucracy" argument.
3. Whether design guidelines were onerous procedurally and financially.

4. The impact of guidelines on noncontributing property.
5. Whether districting concealed an antidevelopment bias or other hidden agendas.
6. Map boundary issues.

Now you might say these issues aren't new to us, that we've seen them in one form or another in our community meetings. And I'd say you're right. But do I have to spell out the advantages for you? Just think:

- We know we've been on the right track in anticipating questions all along.
- We can do subtraction and see which issues we might set aside now.
- We might detect how well our opponents are doing in getting their points across.
- We can gauge how the vote is shaping up before the hearing.

This kind of intelligence will keep us focused on what's important. We can use it in drafting our own mailings. And when the time comes for our testimony, we will have a fair assurance that commissioners who've raised the issues we address will be mentally, not just bodily, in attendance.

And what if the planning staff won't play ball? Well, it's good to know it early on, too. In that case, it'll be up to us to get some kind of clarity about how the meetings will be conducted and the final report crafted.

SETTING THE GROUND RULES

Speak with the commission chairs directly about how they plan on conducting their hearings. This kind of procedural query does not fall under *ex parte* restrictions.

Does the chair plan on taking public sentiment into account? If so, find out whether he or she will be looking for a petition, or will the sampling be broadened to invite any and all comments from the floor? Of course, no chair is likely to rule any citizen's testimony out of order. But the chair may define what is germane, ask the public to stick to it, and instruct fellow commissioners on what's under consideration.

It's a question of the hand on the tiller. Will the chair pursue the most direct course, or will the hearing be allowed to wander wherever public opinion blows it? We ourselves knew to take a firm line in our community meetings. But we shouldn't assume commission chairs will be as clear-sighted and determined.

Of course, any chair may say one thing before the meeting and behave quite differently in the event. This is especially true if opponents toss legal or procedural sand in the commission's eyes. Then, too, a handful of demanding opponents can start the commission backpedaling.

STRATEGIZING OUR PRESENTATION

So even if the chair promises to keep the hearing focused on a narrower range of considerations, it's a good idea to go in prepared with a Plan A and a Plan B:

- **Plan A:** We will develop a presentation keyed to all specific directives and criteria in the commission's charge as explained to us by the chair.
- **Plan B:** We will be ready with a full-blown response to anything our opponents try and the chair permits.

In short, we don't want to get caught carrying the proverbial knife to a gunfight.

But we have a potential problem, depending on how testimony is taken. If we proponents are to speak first, then we need to know in advance if we have a right of rebuttal should our adversaries take off in another direction. If not, then we need to use our testimony to:

- Lay out what we've prepared for Plan A.
- Throw a rope around our opponents.

We'll do this by stating unequivocally what the hearing is about, what is prescribed for consideration by the commission's terms of reference, and *what the chair has specified to us in those terms.* This is the way we interject our own leadership into a proceeding where the commission's leadership may need stiffening.

But be careful: Do it as addressing the audience and stay clear of the political faux pas of reminding commissioners of their duty.

As for *how* to arrange your presentation, let me send you to chapter 32. That chapter is about preparing for the City Council hearing, but its basic advice is applicable here as well.

Much is riding on these commission hearings, but not everything. The City Council has the final say. It may agree or disagree with its advisory commissions. Still, we want the commissions' endorsements, and we value the sense of momentum that favorable votes give us in these first hearings.

Momentum attracts attention. We want Council members to take us seriously. We can't be sure they'll read what we send them. But you may be sure that every one of them will read the local newspaper, and success pulls in the press.

TWENTY-SEVEN

Working with the Press

> There is nothing more deceptive than an obvious fact.
>
> —Sherlock Holmes

People say they don't believe everything they read in the newspaper. But have you ever noticed how a news article will influence the way they see an issue and the questions they ask?

And what's not to believe? The facts? In my experience, reporters usually get facts right. But like the smile on the Mona Lisa, an obvious fact is incomprehensible out of context.

No political issue is ever just about facts. No one more fact, once found, can ever settle a political difference. As we know, politics is about conflicting interests, contesting perspectives, and competing influence among contending parties.

That's what good newspaper stories are about, too. Nailing down a story is like jumping on a moving train: the facts are easy. It's the dynamics that can put you in the hurt box. Reporters know it. When the time comes to move on a story, they have to go with what they know and trust their own judgment.

So each reporter will catch hold of a story from a different angle. That's not bias, per se. It's just the way it works when we try to get a grasp on complex passing events.

Reporters are keen observers and far less likely to be biased than we are as participants. That's why politicians—if they're at all serious—prefer to look to the press to tell them what's going on before they listen to us. Their introduction to our districting effort can't help but be seen through the eyes of the reporter's take on the contest.

So when they read an article on districting, we want it to portray the issues as we see them. We want it to raise questions in their minds that will latch onto our answers.

In brief, we want good press. The only thing worse than bad press *isn't* getting no press at all. It's realizing too late we could've done something about it.

A REPORTER'S INSIGHTS

I've arranged for us to have lunch with Jeff Horseman, a longtime city reporter for *The Capital*, a midsized daily here in Annapolis. Jeff has interviewed me for several preservation stories, and I've learned to trust his fairness and accuracy. So I was pleased when he agreed to speak to us about talking to a reporter to get our story out.

Me: Thanks for taking time to talk with us at lunch today, Jeff.

Jeff: So we're going to turn tables here. I like the idea of being the one who gets interviewed for a change!

Me: How open are you to calls from local activists who want you to do an article on their cause?

Jeff: It depends on how it's presented. I think my best ideas for stories are the ones I find on my own, not those that come from people calling in who want me to do this or that for them. But if we can sit and talk about your concerns, I'm more inclined to be receptive.

Me: Would it be hard to interest you in our districting campaign?

Jeff: I think a historic district initiative is a pretty easy thing to get your average local paper interested in. It's a compelling story. It's very emotional. Property rights are fundamental in this country. People will say, "I paid money for this land and I want to be able to do what I want."

Me: What kinds of mistakes do people like me make at the start?

Jeff: There's a common misconception that we're spouting information out, that we're just collecting information to give to the public.

Me: You're not?

Jeff: The best newspapers do stories about people and communities.

Me: What do you look for?

Jeff: The key to a good story is what I call "the central conflict." The real issues confronting neighborhoods—things like that. Many people don't realize that a paper is a business. If people aren't interested in what we write they won't buy our paper. I want to write stuff that people will read, so I look for a compelling story, stories that people can relate to.

Me: But people look to you for information, too.

Jeff: The reality today, with the Internet and cable news, is that we're not going to be providing breaking news. We survive by putting information in context—writing about real people in plain language to grab attention.

Me: What do you say to the charge that reporters care only about controversy?

Jeff: I hear it all the time. This is what I say: Look, I'm not creating it or trying to stir it up. It's out there. My job is to get it right, be fair, and help people understand it. I want to deliver the story in a way that helps the reader understand the world they live in.

Me: And try to help solve the conflict?

Jeff: If what I do ends up helping, then fine. But if I get involved it jeopardizes my objectivity. It's not that I don't care. But if I advocate one way or another it violates my objectivity and makes me part of the story. That's the last thing I want to do.

Me: So how do you deal with it?

Jeff: I try to be open and receptive. I want to get the story right and be scrupulously fair to the people involved. And accountable—to everyone.

Me: Let's talk about balanced reporting. When you talk about doing a balanced story about a controversy, do you mean by balance that there are two sides to the story or two groups of roughly equal size? What if there are two points of view split, say, 70 percent for one side, 15 percent neutral and the rest on the other side in the community?

Jeff: It's a tricky issue to say how many are on side A and on side B. If it's a ninety-ten split I don't want to say it's fifty-fifty. On the other hand, I don't want to ignore the fact that other people may have different opinions.

Me: So I ought to get you reliable statistics.

Jeff: I want to see a poll, something quantifiable. But absent that, I have to be careful about accepting your word that "most people" are on your side. I have to see the evidence with my own eyes. For instance, I might go to a hearing and see where people stand. But if you say to me, "You know, Jeff, most people want the historic district," you might be right but I have to be careful about writing it. Some people get upset with reporting the other side. They say it clouds the issue or shows bias. But it's not my job to be referee or declare a winner.

Me: Would you trust our petition as evidence of our support?

Jeff: In journalism, there's an old saying. If your mother says she loves you, check it out. I think a reporter would call up a random sample and say, "Hey, this is Jeff Horseman at *The Capital*. I just want to make sure, did you sign this petition?" And find out why. I'd want to make sure I wasn't given phony names and street addresses. It happens. You don't want your evidence in a story to turn up fraudulent and backfire on you. Just make sure your petition is verifiable.

Me: Let's say a group of us has a districting proposal ready and now I'm picking up the phone to call your paper. I want to get our story out. What happens next?

Jeff: The switchboard will probably pass you to the newsroom. Every newspaper operates its own way. You might get the city editor, or the assistant metro editor or you might be sent directly to a reporter. An editor will talk with a reporter later, or the reporter will go to the editor who'll say "go ahead" or "nah, this is part of a larger story we'll do differently."

Me: What if I've read your reporting and liked it? Can I just ask for you?

Jeff: Of course.

Me: What can I say to get you to do the story?

Jeff: Try to put some salesmanship into it. Think about how a reporter has to tell readers, "This is why you ought to care about this." You need to realize that what's important to some people is not necessarily important to a larger group of readers. It's like broccoli. We know we ought to care, but do we?

Me: So how do I pitch it?

Jeff: Don't use big words. The key is simplicity. People want to sound impressive so they'll sound like they know what they're talking about. But I strive every day to kill the jargon. If I hear about—

Me: —"preserving the integrity of the built environment". . . .

Jeff: Yeah, if I hear that, I start mentally checking out—"Oh, no, here we go. . . !" Some people say we dumb down the news by avoiding big words. But I think it's the opposite. When you use one-syllable words you do a better job of explaining to more people.

Me: And they take up less space.

Jeff: I might write twenty, thirty-five, or forty inches for a story and my editor says cut it, condense it. I want to leave crucial information in. And what about this great quote I have? People don't understand this. They complain that I took a complicated issue and oversimplified it. They don't understand that I have to appeal to a broad audience that doesn't care about the details like they do.

Me: So what you're saying is that if we think it's important we should tell it to you in the simplest, most straightforward way possible.

Jeff: With a lot of interesting detail and a lot of simplicity that will hook the reader from the beginning to the end.

Me: Say I've got you interested. Do you want me to send you materials before we talk, or talk first?

Jeff: Charts, graphs, testimonials—they're helpful once I decide to do the story. First we'll talk. I like to do my interviews face-to-face. The people I interview are more comfortable with me in person. The phone is too impersonal. I always, always want to go knock on doors.

Me: Do you expect a press release from us? If we don't have one, will we look amateurish? If we do, will we appear too slick?

Jeff: I don't expect anything. A press release, prepared statement, whatever, is no indication of your credibility or standing. As a journalist in my community, anyone can call me and I'll treat everyone equally. There's an ethic here that Joseph Pulitzer stated well. He said that we should be a voice for the voiceless. That means to tell the untold story. Representing all aspect of the community is part of the creativity and satisfaction of the job.

Me: Do you think reporters favor the underdog? If we're fighting big property developers, are we the underdog, or is the underdog the retiree who's afraid of historic districting?

Jeff: I try to present the whole picture. It comes down to communication. I'd be off base if I tried to talk only about the big, overarching issues that don't seem to affect anyone in particular, or if I only wrote about the little grandmother being pressured by preservationists.

Me: When we meet, do you want a presentation from me, or do you want an interview?

Jeff: A conversation. I'll probably start with, "OK, tell me why you're doing this." I want you to do most of the talking.

Me: Would you prefer to talk with two or three of us to get varying interests and perspectives?

Jeff: Every reporter has a preference. I prefer one-on-one. It all depends. A conversation is harder to do with more in a room. A panel discussion bouncing ideas around can be good, too, if a reporter can stay with it.

Me: What's the ideal interview, or conversation?

Jeff: It's one in which you can get someone away from pat, safe answers and move to the heart of the issue. So I want to do my homework and ask insightful questions. When I do this, some people think I'm trying to trick them into saying something offensive. No, I'm just trying to find out where they're coming from and get an honest story.

Me: What's your pet peeve?

Jeff: "I want this to be a *positive* story." If you say that, it indicates to me you don't understand my job. But people often tell me they want the story to make them or their program look good. We're not in the business of making people look good or bad, building up or tearing down. My job is to look for the truth, get the facts, be comprehensive, and write it in a way that's easy to read. I want to be able to say, "OK, folks, this is your world."

Me: Let's assume then it'll just be the two of us in the conversation. Do I talk off the record or on?

Jeff: Assume I'll use everything you say.

Me: But what if I don't want my name in print?

Jeff: It'll hurt your case. If you have the courage to call up the paper then you should stand up for the article. People have this idea that reporters use lots of anonymous sources. We don't like them. If someone says they don't want to be quoted, I get skeptical. "Well, why don't you?" I think. If you've got a good reason, like a boss's policy, I can work with that. Talk to me on background, then, but direct me to people who'll talk on the record. It's not all or nothing.

Me: What else do I need to do?

Jeff: Preservation is a good story. It's not hard to sell it to an editor. It's very emotional. It deals with interesting problems in a community.

Me: What if your editor has already taken a position on the historic district? Is there pressure on you?

Jeff: None whatsoever. My newsroom editor isn't the editorial page editor. Editorials are usually written after the story appears. My job is to tell the story. An editorial is to get the debate started.

Me: So how should I time my call? Just before a hearing, or sooner than that?

Jeff: An upcoming hearing in a couple of days will be a point of interest to readers. We tell them about the hearing and tell them what it's about. But a longer lead is a good idea—a week or longer. You've got a chance at being a front-page Sunday story. People can read a longer story and get a better base of knowledge.

Me: So something doesn't have to be happening right now?

Jeff: The more time you can give a reporter the better the story will be. You need to realize that reporters are juggling two or three or more different stories on deadline.

Me: Let's say I give you a long lead. What if you want to call the Mayor or members of the City Council but I'm afraid they'll stake out a position before I've had a chance to influence them?

Jeff: You need to be very clear if you want me to keep it under wraps. I want to write this story and I'm not going to let anyone tell me when. But I might agree to hold off if you give me a good idea of when we can run it. But you can't say, "Write on this, but don't call that person." No editor would agree to that. And I won't agree to let you see a copy of it before it goes to press.

Me: We have three hearings coming up. Can I get three stories, one before each meeting?

Jeff: All depends. "Can we get three?" That's not the approach. Toss your ideas out and let the paper decide if it's worth a second or third story.

Me: Will you be telling me if you're talking with the opposition and give me a chance to rebut?

Jeff: Not necessarily. You have to expect I'll try to get the other side. If you ask me, I'll tell you. But don't expect me to call and tell you who's getting interviewed. If some developer calls you a NIMBY [not in my backyard] moron and I might use the quote, it's a courtesy to tell you first.

Me: If I ask will you tell me what the opposition is saying and doing? Can you be a source of intelligence about them?

Jeff: You mean, like what a developer says? I don't mind telling you what's common knowledge or on the record. But if you want me to predict what's coming down the road, that sort of thing . . . I'm more reticent.

Me: How about what you know about the City Council or one of the commissions? A little quid pro quo, you might say. When I'm talking to you about our plans, would you answer questions I have about what you've seen, who is who, how they might respond to our issue? Can we have a two-way conversation?

Jeff: The last thing I want to be seen as on my beat is a power broker. If I wanted influence I'd run for office. But I might respond to specific questions as long as I'm not burning my other sources and you're asking about public knowledge. But basically, ethically, I can't get involved.

Me: How much do you think local officials are influenced by your articles?

Jeff: [Smiling.] I've been told we have a lot of influence. But reporters aren't deliberately trying to influence City Hall. That would affect their credibility. Officials read the paper to find out what's happening.

Me: What kinds of mistakes can I make with you that'll hurt me?

Jeff: Shopping the story around to the competition. That strikes me as manipulative, playing people off against each other. Of course, if I think a competitor might print it first, I might want the story. But it's not a good idea to try it.

Me: What else?

Jeff: If you don't like the story I write don't call and say, "Jeff, you idiot! This is totally wrong!" You can catch more flies with honey than vinegar. I'm going to be much more receptive to working with you if you say, "Jeff, you missed this point. Let me explain how." If you come in with guns blazing I'm not going to be receptive. Reporters are people. The more you're aware of the pressures they face, the more they'll work with you.

Me: And?

Jeff: Don't lie. My credibility is important. If I find out I've been snowed, if you've handed me a lot of BS, I'm not going to believe you again. Every day I put something with my byline in the paper people are going to judge me. There are a lot of people out there who like to see reporters get screwed.

After that, I figured I couldn't very well stick him with my lunch tab. So I thanked Jeff again, said goodbye, and picked over my tortilla chips along with something I'd heard. Once the story appears, an editorial may follow. So once you've put your story out, go see the folks at the editorial page and sell them on your civic vision.

TWENTY-EIGHT

A Civic Vision

> There is no substitute for a clear vision and a decisive direction.
>
> —Dick Morris

As a reporter, Jeff told us that he looks for the "central conflict" in a community story and aims at being "scrupulously fair to the people involved." That's balanced reporting. So we have to wonder: How will we come across to his readers—on balance?

Imagine what will happen when Jeff goes after the story. Our opponents will stress their pivotal issue: property rights. And what will we do? Take him on an eye-opening walk of the neighborhood? Of course we will. And he'll report it as he sees it.

So what will official decision makers take away from his story? Next to property rights, our issues may sound a bit precious. These days, like it or not, rights talk is presumptively, well, right. If we're to win them over, we should give Jeff the story of grassroots leadership that has forged a new sense of community in the midst of conflict.

"JUST AUTHORITY" AND THE PUBLIC GOOD

Conservative columnist David Brooks of the *New York Times* points the way. He has affirmed that good government is about more than liberty. It is about *just* authority.

What does that mean to us? Well, obviously the historic district will establish a new *authority* over how we exercise our property rights as free citizens. We know that this authority is *legal*. But what is it that makes it *just*?

When we put together our practical vision we took pains to justify district designation in terms of property owner interests. That is no longer enough.

Our target audience has changed. The decision makers we seek to win over don't have property-based interests in the district. In fact, if they did they'd have to recuse themselves.

Of course they'll want to know, and we should tell them, why a majority of property owners sides with us. Still, numbers aren't enough—and for a good reason. A majority calculating their own interests can be wrongheaded. Our form of representative government holds that elected officials are better situated than the self-involved people themselves to judge the connection between self-interest and the public good—and to protect and advance the latter.

So what is it about the historic district that is in the public good—and thus *just*—beyond our practical vision? What can we say for it so that it can hold its own against property rights claims?

For this we need a new sort of vision—a *civic vision*—that ties the interests of City leaders to what we've already achieved in our community. Instead of simply advocating preservation and its benefits, let's give them a *leadership investment* in our initiative and make them complicit in our success.

SEEING THE CIVIC COMMUNITY

Now let's get Jeff—or rather our own local reporter—back in here. A great thing about reporters is they don't like getting bogged down in details. We can tell him about the "preservation-plus" approach we've used and avoid the quicksand of technicalities. Those details, we may confidently say, are well-known and accepted by our supporters. We've got their signatures to prove it.

So have our allies all become preservationists? No, of course not.

"Ahh," comes the response. "They're in your chorus now, but when the time comes for the regulations to apply to them they'll be singing a different tune. That's what I'm hearing at City Hall."

And that's a most dangerous critique, if it's coming from commissioners or elected officials. As they see it, we're asking them to make law on the basis of an insubstantial and transitory confluence of interests. Oh, they'll accept that everyone is pro-preservation after their own fashion, at least for now. But experience has taught them to doubt that our neighbors really, truly want more regulations. "They ought to be careful what they wish for," they'll say. And public officials know they'll be the ones to take the fall if folks turn on the district later on. Can you blame them? In the land of electoral politics and political appointments, it's always CYA time.

We haven't come this far to smile and say, "But that's what they want, Scout's honor." So let's go right into the teeth of their argument.

We want to make it crystal clear that we're talking about *districting* here, not just *preservation*, and so are our supporters. Our reporter has probably heard breakers claim that there's not much around here worth preserving, or something like that. Well, we disagree. But that's not where the real story is. And that's surely not the only thing our City leaders should be looking at. So here's our pitch.

The truth is, in most of our communities, *what's preserved isn't nearly as impressive as the rare quality of civic life seen in the very fact of citizens caring for a legacy*—any legacy no matter how common.

Here's how I see it. The outward appearance of a historic district reflects the internal health of a community. Long-standing features of the built environment are touchstones of civic memory, reminding us that what we do lives on after us. A community that cares for its past by districting, then, is a community dedicated to being responsible for its own future. A historic district says to us, "This is a place to invest our lives, to raise a family, to grow a business, to retire in security."

Getting to the point where a community petitions for district designation is quite a civic accomplishment. Isn't this, we should ask, the ideal toward which all political leadership aspires?

That's it, then. Three short paragraphs to refocus attention from conflict to what visionary leadership can achieve in community building.

SHARING OUR SUCCESS

We know that ideological fights over property rights can make decision makers shy. So we need to stand firmly for action, not talk, deeds and not principles that lead to a better community.

Our basic conviction is that sound communities can't be achieved by standing on abstract principles—especially if those principles give folks an excuse for acting irresponsibly. Principles of freedom are the foundation of free government. And free government holds that *when the citizenry is self-governed enough to do good*

*things, those things should be encoded in law and supported by insti-
tutions equal to the task.* That is how just authority arises.

Leadership is about context, then, about inspiring and facilitating good acts and securing them in public practice. Ronald Reagan
understood the point. He told *60 Minutes* that "the greatest leader
is not the one who does the greatest things, but the one who gets
the people to do the greatest things."

Public officials should be satisfied that our neighbors see the
historic district as a great gift to themselves. *And they should be
proud that it has taken place on their watch, at the time of their leadership.*

So everywhere we go, every public chance we get, let's congrat-
ulate our City leaders on having nurtured a community in which
average folks like you and me have been inspired to bring a winning
proposal like ours before them for ratification. Let's speak in celebration of the opportunity to join together with them in the final
stages of this exceptional achievement.

Make it a main theme in what you say to your reporter, what you
put in a guest column, and what you submit to editorial writers. Put
it on your website. Emphasize it wherever you speak and *make sure
our City leaders know it.*

Our goal is to raise the level of discourse in the community. Reporters' good instincts may seek out the "central conflict." But
don't let them miss the new and vital awareness of community that
we've brought out of that conflict.

The big human interest story isn't about the penurious resident
who fears districting. The real story is about how regular folks
around the corner got off their duffs and inspired their neighbors to
uncommon accomplishment.

Back when we put together our *practical vision* we joined the
particular interests of individual neighbors with our own. Our *civic
vision* now proclaims that the sum is greater than its parts: the historic district is in the common interest of everyone even if some in-

dividuals with particular interests don't yet acknowledge it. If the concept of the common good has any validity at all, then it's to be found in that kind of public policy.

You won't need to remind decision makers that this is about more than public policy, either. We're not just designating a district here. We're keeping accounts and selecting future leaders.

To deny the district would be to deny the best in us—their constituents—and cheapen their records. They should see there's no future in going there.

That's not just a civic vision. That's a promise.

THE PROBLEM

But will decision makers recognize the public good when they see it? And seeing it, will they know what to do with it—and have the political courage to see it through?

Those questions ought to interest the editorial writers at your local paper, too. But you know what? It's a shame we have to pose them. So, next, let's consider why.

TWENTY-NINE

The Politics of Public Hearings

Everybody lies, but it doesn't matter since nobody listens.

—Lieberman's Law

City Mayors and Council members aren't disinterested judges of merit. They are for the most part biased listeners who have been rewarded for their biases by getting elected. Most of them want to do it again next time.

Can you blame them? The electoral process being what it is, they have to be creatures of interests—their own and others'. They don't want to know about the historic district nearly as much as they are attuned to a question as old as politics itself: *Cui bono?* Who benefits?

You and I already have an answer. It's all to the public good, we like to say.

But the common good, the public interest, is hard to see from where they sit. Of course, not every public official is nearsighted. Some are truly devoted to doing the right thing. They're the ones who take time to listen and study. They ask good questions and sift through the evidence. They engage their colleagues on substance. Such officials do exist. I hope you'll find one or more on your City Council. If you have a majority, call *Ripley's Believe It or Not.* Even then bear in mind that the public hearing format of Council meetings isn't conducive to taking the longer view of things, either.

These meetings are very much in the moment, with all the emotionally charged Sturm und Drang of community fights—though with much of the feeling of community stripped away by the proceedings. Testimony is a rat-a-tat-tat of rights versus regulations, "he said," "she said," "ifs," "ands," and "buts." Time presses, and there's likely more on their agenda than just us. They are perhaps perturbed that we haven't settled this thing on our own. They wonder how they can solve it if we can't.

A QUESTION OF LEADERSHIP

"We don't have a clear mandate" for designation, the Southern Mayor concluded at the end of a hearing described as "both tedious and confusing."

And whose fault was that? Long months of hard work were lost because historic district proponents failed to exercise the leadership needed to get the vote. In a hard-fought districting contest, winning the vote depends on creating a political environment in which decision makers are motivated by their interests to vote with us.

So what's this "mandate" thing about, anyway? Think a minute. When did you last hear a politician use the word *mandate?* I'll bet it wasn't to say, "I don't have one. My hands are tied." We're used to hearing mandates claimed on the thinnest of pretexts, aren't we? Sure we are. *Leaders* claim mandates and then spend whatever political capital they have to press ahead with favored legislation. What the Mayor was pointing to wasn't the absence of a mandate. It was the Council's own lack of a *will to lead.*

Elected officials prefer to be pushed toward a decision that finds general favor. "We want something everybody can feel good about," a Council member said in similar circumstances. But if the Council is looking for a mandate in "feel-good" solutions then they're not thinking in terms of public policy. They're looking for palliatives. You and I have to lead them to a better result.

AN INAUSPICIOUS SETTING

Unlucky for us, City Council proceedings are not well designed to produce a distinguished outcome. Here's how it typically works. The chair of the HPC or the Planning Department presents the draft proposal. The floor is opened for sworn public comment from anyone wishing to be heard. Public testimony is then closed and the question is turned over to Council members for an exchange— rarely a real discussion—among themselves leading toward a vote.

When it's our turn to speak in the process, we are asked to give our name and address for the record and then state our interest. That's it. No prologue, no follow-up. We get to say anything we want. And, too bad for us, our opponents usually do.

Any progress we might have made on issues in our community meetings doesn't help us much here with the opposition. Once the hearing begins they will revert to the same canards, the same red herrings, the same distortions—that is, the same discrediting tactics that they started with on day one. They'll try to flood the hearing with accusations, complaints, and appeals to property rights. Their goal is to create the appearance of an unholy mess of disagreements in the community.

So now what? Do we have to fight the fight all over again?

That's why Lieberman's observation is a comfort. It tells us to take it easy. Sworn testimony or no, everyone knows our opponents are lying—or playing fast and loose with the truth. But then everyone assumes that we are, too. Still, no sweat. Nobody's paying attention anyway.

Is that so? Don't just take it from me. A past county commissioner suggests I title this chapter, "The Art of Not Listening." Former Missoula mayor and speaker of the Montana state legislature Daniel Kemmis has written in *Community and the Politics of Place* that public hearings "are curiously devoid of that very quality which their name might seem to imply."[1]

The right of every citizen to be heard is also an equal right to be ignored. Those who testify have no obligation to respect, much less engage, each other's views. And once public testimony is closed, Council members will generally care less for puzzling through what is said than for finding some way out of the impasse before midnight.

Talk is about policy. That's on the surface. But calculating political interests is far easier for elected officials than sorting out and weighing conflicting testimonies.

We are not strangers to the sway that interests hold over ideas. We rose in stature as community leaders by drawing our neighbors' interests into our practical vision. But we may feel mighty puny as we arrive at City Hall, where other leaders with other interests rule, and the reality of the hearing room sets in.

Matt Damon's freshman trial lawyer in *The Rainmaker* knows the feeling. He has the law, his case, and the evidence down pat. And still, on that first day he tells us, "I look around the courtroom and I know I haven't even been born yet."

CHANGING OUR STRATEGY

The way Council procedures are supposed to produce policy reminds me of what Woodrow Wilson once said about golf. What we call golf, he said, is a game in which you try to put a small ball in a small hole with instruments wholly unsuited to the task.

So what can we do if the Council is going to give us a sub-par round? We can't refuse to play the game, and they're not going to change the rules just because we ask them. You play your ball where it lies—but you're not without options. You may change that one part of the proceedings that you control: your testimony.

Council proceedings are set up for us to testify to our interests. Changing our testimony means changing the interests that we want the Council to consider. What I have in mind, then, is a significant change of strategy. We will speak to the Council's own interest in finding their way to a defensible vote.

We will, of course, advocate the district. It would be disorienting if we didn't. But we're not going to engage our opponents and argue it from scratch. We've been there, done that, got the T-shirt.

We have already brought our neighbors to a decision that is as good as it gets. So let's give the Council that decision, back it up with our testimony, and show them the style of leadership that will enable them to make it their own.

OUR TESTIMONY

We'll speak their language of partnerships and alliances and show them the coalition of supporters we've put together in the district. We will talk, too, about synergies between the district and the larger community—the symbiotic interplay among historic resources, private and public places, business interests, nonprofit activities, cultural and recreational opportunities. All this will put them on notice that they'll be disappointing a broader coalition of interests than just ours in preservation if they fail us.

That is the lead-in to our other argument. We will assert that the community itself has done all the sorting out, the balancing of interests, the brokering of agreements that may be expected. On our own, we led our neighbors through an open, inclusive, and fairly conducted decision-making process. Call it an exercise in direct democracy, if you like. Property owners have met and talked, contended and reasoned together in different venues.

Along the way we established a practical vision that succeeded in quickening a new civic sense among many of our neighbors. We found common ground as we worked together, and together we took responsibility for our neighborhood.

Many who joined our campaign have become newly optimistic about local government. Try as we might, we'll say, we could not persuade everybody that politics is about more than just isolating themselves from the public interest and defending themselves from government.

As it turned out there was enough community feeling to make winning the decision for districting possible and enough of its absence to make designation necessary.

The results of our efforts, like votes, are registered in our petition. This long, deliberative process has produced a responsible decision that—with all due respect to the Council—is quite likely a better decision than any that might be reached in Council chambers in an hour or so.

THE SOLUTION

Our strategy, then, will be to insist—with all the influence that our standing in the community gives us—that the political question before the Council isn't whether the historic district should be approved. The real question is *whether the Council is going to accept and validate the community's decision.*

And what are the Council's interests in this? Right now, we are offering them something that is as close to a mandate as they are likely to find. It is the solution they are looking for to bring the proceedings to an efficient close with a show of decisive leadership.

Our solution offers them a ready-made, uncomplicated way to justify their vote to anyone who may pick them apart later. *Justify*, not simply explain. A vote for the district is more than a vote for one side over another. It is a *vote for community in the midst of conflict*. It is a vote for the public good as the public—the people—have come to see it. So it is also the right thing to do.

ACTING IN ADVANCE

We have one issue left to address: timing. Council members will have at least a fair idea of how they'll vote before the hearing begins. And a made-up mind is a terrible thing to chase.

So how do we get to them first? Through lobbying. We don't know, until you find out, whether you can meet one-on-one with HPC and Planning commissioners. But you should be able to speak to each Council member. Pay special attention to the Mayor and the Council member from your own district.

Assume what you say will get back to our opponents. But if we hold off till the public hearing, we run the risk of saying too little too late.

Just keep in mind that you don't get to take a mulligan, to call do-overs in politics. So before you head down to City Hall, let's get some pointers on how to do it from an experienced lobbyist.

NOTE

1. Daniel Kemmis, *Community and the Politics of Place*, Norman: University of Oklahoma Press, 1990, p. 54.

THIRTY

A Conversation with a Lobbyist

> Here's to plain speaking and clear understanding.
>
> —Sydney Greenstreet, *The Maltese Falcon*

We are sitting in the back room of a political speakeasy on the outskirts of Washington, D.C. Just the two of us in comfortable chairs, drinks in hand, talking politics.

He's a successful lobbyist who has agreed to talk about his craft. He prefers to remain anonymous so he can be candid. I'll just call him "Sam."

Like many lobbyists, Sam has also had a career in law. In recent years, though, it's been politics. He has spent twelve years lobbying and three and a half being lobbied. Walked both sides of the street in fair weather and foul. His conservative credentials are sterling and he has lived in a historic district. Liked it, too. Mostly.

I set the stage by explaining that we're expecting a Council fight over our historic district. We think a little lobbying is in order and would like some pointers.

In the momentary silence that follows as he gathers his thoughts, I swear I hear Sydney Greenstreet say to Bogie, "Now, sir, we'll talk if you like. I'll tell you outright, I'm a man who likes talking to a man who likes to talk."

THE DIALOGUE

Me: What's the best way to approach an elected official?

Sam: Find someone to make an introduction for you. Let them send a note and say, "My friend Bill is going to call you and wants to come by and really needs to see you." If you want to see the Mayor, that might get you a "Hi, Bill. This is Mary, my assistant. I wanted to meet you but I've got another meeting. She'll take notes and brief me today about what's going on." Where there's no staff, just the official, it's harder for them to give you the slip.

Me: Are you saying they'd just as soon not meet with me?

Sam: It's really all about maximizing their time. It's like this: staffers or other people I trust are extensions of me. They help me see and talk to more people and accomplish more of what I'm supposed to be doing.

Me: So what do I say when we meet?

Sam: Lobbying to me is a matter of priorities. Know your subject backwards and forwards. If you're going to give them printed material, know and be able to explain every word in it.

Me: And second...?

Sam: Know this person so you can walk in and say, "Well, Alderwoman Smith, I saw your last three votes on the environment and that was a good piece of work." They love that, you know.

Visit their websites. Find the topics that have made these people jump up and do things.

Me: So you're telling me to schmooze them!

Sam: If you come in the door and start saying, "We've got a historic district pending," their eyes are going to glaze over. They'll say, "OK, just give me your literature and I'll see you later." But if you walk in the front door and say, "I understand you had a charity golf tournament the other day? How did you do?" "Aw," he says, "I just go out and have my picture taken with the donors and hit a few balls. But I can tell you I came that close to a hole in one." And now you're in. Call it what you want, but we're talking by that point.

Me: What else?

Sam: If you walk into an elected official's office and don't know how they've voted in the past, *shame on you!* If he's voted against your issues, you want to be able to say, "I know your record and it's important to me to know why you voted that way." You'll find out pretty quickly where he stands with you.

Me: Then what do you do?

Sam: You're getting to the point where you can say, "Let me tell you what makes our proposal different." Talk about substance, and address how technicalities might get worked out. If that doesn't move them, then say, "If you can tell me something we can fix, something we can make better that would bring you on-board, that's what I want to hear. Let me try to work with you on this." If you go in there with this completely adversarial "you and I don't agree and you've always voted against us" attitude, then don't waste your time. You'll just make them mad. But if you go in there with the idea that you really want to figure out what the problem is, then *that* makes you a very valuable player in their eyes.

CHAPTER THIRTY

Me: What do you do if they agree with you but still say they can't vote for you?

Sam: They can say that you make perfectly good sense. But then, if they're candid, they might tell you they have other commitments and can't vote for you. It's not easy for them to look you in the eye and tell you no. When that happens, I say, "Thank you for being direct. I admire your refreshing candor. It's been a pleasure." Stand, shake hands, and leave.

Me: Just like that, it's over?

Sam: Sometimes you just have to know you're going to lose that vote and have to move on. But never burn a bridge. Treat them well and with respect, and they'll know they owe you one.

Me: Do you ever lean on them, threaten them with political repercussions?

Sam: If you're part of the Soprano family you shouldn't be a lobbyist. That's just not going to get it. Still, you have to show them why it's in their interest to vote with you. Have your statistics perfect—that impresses them. If you can tell them how their vote will affect them, they'd be fools not to listen to you. I have seen people with steam coming out of their ears talking to people they wouldn't choose to talk to, yet saying to themselves, "I need this. This is an education. I'm listening to another portion of what's going on in this town and I need to understand it."

Me: What mistakes can I make?

Sam: Never lie. Never tell any elected official anything that isn't absolutely true. You have only one chance in this business, *one lie*, and they'll never listen to you again because they can't depend on you. And nobody will be able to repair the damage you do to your cause.

Me: Do we talk about our opponents or just stick to our message?

Sam: You need to tell the person what the opposition to your proposal is going to be, and you need to be deadly honest with them. No sugar coating. If they end up getting hit in the back of the head when they're not looking by something you didn't tell them you won't be welcomed back.

Me: So we show them the downside, too.

Sam: You go in and say, "I want you to do A, and if you do A you're going to be hearing from this group of folks. They're going to come in and yell and scream at you. But let me tell you why you're going to be better off in the long run for being with us on this issue."

Me: What should I take in with me?

Sam: Suppose they say, "That's a very interesting point. Do you have any facts you can leave with me?" I usually go armed with one-page talking papers on major topics that I can put in their hand.

Me: How detailed?

Sam: Short. Bulleted. This is a one-shot deal. Not even complete sentences. Less than one page. My phone number on each page at the bottom. "Call me," I say, "and I'll give you a blowout on it." If I can get a screwdriver under the lid of the paint can and start popping it up—enough so I can slide some fact papers in there with them—now I'm doing something.

Me: Will they tell me where they stand before I leave?

Sam: Most of them—the smart ones—will never tell you they're going to vote one way and then go and vote another. They'll simply not commit while you're there. You'll hear "Thank you and now let me go back and look at this." That gives you a perfect opportunity to say, "Well, let me help you. Give me an e-mail address where I can send you more information if you need it."

Me: Does money buy influence?

Sam: Not since campaign contributions have been restricted. So I've got to be a good talker, a good presenter.

Me: What defeats you?

Sam: Sometimes I watch the vote and wonder how that person could vote against me. They can be sincerely with you, yet vote where their constituents are. If you let yourself get upset about that, then you'll end up against our whole system of government. They're just being smart. That clue tells me that when I walk in their door, at the very least I have to know something about their constituents.

Me: But our historic district is probably going to be limited to the geography of only one Council member's district.

Sam: You'd be surprised. Put together some "well whaddya know?!" facts. A historic district in one place might be the balance needed to secure rezoning for business in another. If you can make that kind of link, you can go in a say, "Hey, this will be good for you, too." Be specific. Use examples from other cities if you have to. Get them thinking that there *are* advantages for them, too. "By golly," they'll say, "I can vote for that."

Me: Why do they always seem to want a compromise?

Sam: That's the way politics works. They know that policy differences never get fully resolved. So pulling to the middle is what it's all about. If you get to the middle you win.

Me: Do you go in alone or take others with you?

Sam: Depends on the situation. If it's a technical issue, I'll take a specialist along. I don't want to be caught talking about something outside my area of expertise.

Me: Do you ever coordinate with other groups or associations?

Sam: Good question. I handle what I can do best. If I anticipate prejudice against me because of my client or my issue, I might ask someone else, like the Chamber of Commerce, to go in with me and speak to our issue. I'll be a follower and they'll say this isn't just about preservation. There are other interests involved and they're here to talk about them.

Me: How do I know when to leave?

Sam: That reminds me. I've got a trip to Texas tomorrow and I still haven't packed my bags. . . . See? You'll know when it's time to go. *But don't you push it.* Don't pop in and pop out again. Don't just say your piece and leave. They'll wonder, "What was *that* all about?" Maybe their questions don't get answered. Maybe they don't even know what those questions are when you walk in the door. Give them time to think while you're there. Look, if the guy seems to be in no hurry, then spend some time getting to know each other on a personal level. It puts a human face on your issue.

Me: How soon do we go see them?

Sam: As early as possible. Get them your materials. Start telling them why this district is important to them. Give them time to get a handle on the pros and cons and then go back again. *Get that door propped open for further contact.* Ask them, "Where do we need to go on this? What do I need to do to make you comfortable with this? Can you give me some direction?" That way, you're taking them seriously *and* getting yourself invited back.

Me: How likely are they to make up their minds before the public hearing?

Sam: Some won't have their minds made up. But the ideal of the hearing, where ideas and positions are exchanged and decided, is not the way it works in America today. Everybody has access to all the information they need without having to listen to speeches. If they like what they hear from you they'll be repeating it at the hearing.

Me: How important is good press?

Sam: Everyone reads the paper, maybe has a clipping service. If there's an article on a meteor falling in Farmer Jones's field today, tomorrow there will be a hearing on "Meteors: What We Can Do about Them." The news is of critical importance to them.

Me: Final thoughts?

Sam: Do you know the movie *The Music Man*? It opens with a train coming into River City carrying traveling salesmen singing about selling. They all agree on one thing. As the train comes into the station, they're singing in rhythm with the slowing pistons, "You've got to know the terr-i-tory." Well, you have to know how politics is played. It takes a lot of effort. You can't just jump up, jam your finger into the air, and say, "I'm going to change this!" Folks will come down on you like a ton of bricks. It takes knowing how the game is played. And if you can't play the game you've got no business doing this.

Me: So we've been told.

With that he says he *really* is going to Texas and has to pack. We put away our glasses. We step out into the night. A chill mist has blown into town. As we shake hands I can't help but think, "So that's the stuff that votes are made of."

THIRTY-ONE

A Checklist for One-on-One Meetings

Come, give us a taste of your quality.

—William Shakespeare, *Hamlet*

The moment has come to keep your appointments with our elected officials. This is your best chance to show them who you are. So are you ready?

Here's a checklist to help you get squared away. Most of it should be obvious by now.

1. **Work your contacts.** Have your reputation precede you. Get the introductions that will make the Mayor or Council member look forward to meeting with you. Ask a well-connected supporter or shaper to place a phone call. Check with national, state, and local preservation groups for influential intermediaries.

2. **Know the territory.** This is the land of politics. You will be having a political discussion that has political objectives. Don't push them to agree with you on preservation if they'll vote with us for other reasons.

3. **Suit up for the game.** Become them. Look and act the part. There are two kinds of intelligence: the kind you gather and the kind you show. You want them to say to themselves, "Well now, there's more to this than I suspected. Maybe this can work for me, too." Intractable issues are sometimes decided on the basis of personalities. The more appealing party can get the vote.

4. **Go with others.** As Clint Eastwood said in *Pale Rider*, "a man alone is easy prey." Especially if you're a political novice. Take along two or three people who know which end is up. Divvy up the presentation and rehearse it. Be ready to bail each other out of tight spots.

5. **Know your subject.** Think *inside* the box and *know that box*. You're looking for fluency in focused arguments. Stay on message. No invention and no speculation. Don't talk about what you don't know. Remember Molly Ivins's advice: If you get in a hole, stop digging.

6. **Don't personalize issues.** By now the politics of personality are in full swing. Don't use opponents' names to characterize issues. It will make them memorable and make you sound petty.

7. **Know your policy maker.** It's smart and courteous to know your host. Assess the relative influence of the Mayor and each Council member. See where the likely swing votes are. Find out what is important to them and focus on that.

8. **Look them in the eye.** Watch how they respond to you. See when to move on. If you get stuck, island-hop. Move on to the next topic. What was a sticking point may be resolved in the process.

9. **Listen.** Don't just tell them what *you* think is important. Make sure you understand their point of view. They know best where the levers are to move the vote.

10. **Be positive.** Expect to win. Reframe negative questions and comments in a constructive manner. Don't blame others and don't make points at someone else's expense. Be for, not against. Talk of possibilities, not problems.

11. **Focus on their interests.** What does the historic district mean for them as politicians and as elected officials? What does it mean for the City at large? Don't leave them thinking you don't appreciate their needs. Explore compromises.

12. **Keep your rhetoric cool.** Lose your temper and the district will flicker out like your last match on a windy night. Don't rise to incitements and don't debate—you can't win. They have the power to designate the district, and that trumps anything you think you've got. Say nothing you'll regret the next day.

13. **Be brief.** You have a perishable claim on their attention. Dick Morris says that any political idea can conveyed in thirty seconds. Even a minute is no time for minutiae. Make a point and then move on to the next one.

14. **Avoid jargon and technicalities.** Don't show off what you know about preservation and its more arcane concepts. Speak simply and clearly to sell the district.

15. **Have your talking points ready.** Talking points should be dual use: to convey content and to have the desired political effect. Give them concepts and facts to side with you. Supply them with the words, phrases, and statements that they can use.

16. **Have one-page position papers in hand.** Preface them with an executive summary of the origins of the effort, main objectives, points of contention, community meetings and

due process, and reasons for voting yes. Have briefing papers ready on such basics as:

- The legal basis of historic districts.
- A glossary of regulatory terms: list of work activities,
  design guidelines, certificate of approval.
- Justification of the district's geographical boundaries.
- The chronology of our community notifications and
  meetings.
- Documentation of outreach to our opposition.

Coordinate your materials with other information packets
(see chapter 25). Include a copy of the FAQs document
you distributed in the community. Have your contact information on every page, including your website.

17. **Tell them your story.** Brief them on how we reinvigorated
    a sense of civic pride and responsibility in the community.
    Show them how voters have come to say yes to districting.

18. **Give them a heads-up on the downside.** Help them re-
    duce their exposure and manage negative fallout from vot-
    ing for us. Tell them the juice is worth the squeeze.

19. **Invite them on a tour of the district.** Put a face on your
    district, a living dimension to your proposal. This will
    make an abstraction a concrete reality for them.

20. **Put a hyphen in your conversation when you leave.**
    Don't expect a commitment yet. Keep the door propped
    open. Find a way to stay in touch. Then follow up.

21. **Thank them.** As we'll hear in the next chapter, few people
    remember to thank politicians for their work. Be the ex-
    ception, and make it sincere. After all, the words *polite* and
    politics share the same root, and being polite is politic.

Bear in mind that their time is valuable. Follow Big Dan Teague's
rule in *O Brother, Where Art Thou?* "The one thing you don't want
is air in the conversation."

THIRTY-TWO

Our Public Hearing Presentation

Avoid any specific discussion of public policy at public meetings.

—Cicero

A public hearing is like a trial by ordeal. It is less about a search for truth or the facts in evidence than how we survive it. So let's plan to get it over with quickly.

I don't think the City Council is looking forward to it either. They are used to presentations running on and on as citizens parade to the microphone to say their piece one after another. You can be sure that if we discipline our presentation they'll be grateful.

What's there to lose anyway? As a practical matter, we may assume that most opportunities to win their support will have been seized or missed before we walk into the Council chamber.

We've met one-on-one with Council members and the Mayor and given them information packets. We've invited them to tour the district. We have, I trust, favorable reports from the HPC and

Planning Commission. The newspaper has covered us. Letters and e-mails have been written and phone calls placed.

What better way is there to demonstrate our leadership in the community than to exercise it now in the public hearing? We can do this briefly and, so, impressively.

GETTING TO BINGO

As I'm considering this I run into Bob Agee, our City Administrator, and he couldn't agree more. "Always do that," he tells me. "Avoid redundancy." He has spent years in Council meetings and says that "the one thing that'll just drive you crazy is hearing the same thing over and over and over again. Soon you stop hearing anything, even when new points are interjected."

The core of our presentation must be a unified message delivered in a political narrative that quickly puts on the record:

- This is why the district deserves overlay protection.
- This is the practical vision that's won over property owners.
- This is the civic community that has arisen in the midst of conflict.
- This is what the district will mean for the rest of the City.
- This is what it can help Council members do.
- This is what they can do for it: *vote yes.*

That's your outline. Mix in whatever specific issues motivate Council members. They'll be ticking them off as you speak. You want each of them to get to "Bingo!" as fast as possible.

I'll leave the details to you and your steering committee. You've become the masters of your local situation.

And that's the way I want you to present yourself to decision makers. When you speak to them speak as leader to leader. Show them you know what you are doing, that you've grown accustomed to success in the community and that you expect to win.

PROCEDURAL QUESTIONS

Check out how the City Council conducts hearings. Will we have to sign up to speak, and when? In what order will speakers be taken? First come first served? Or will it be proponents first and opponents later? What is established Council practice?

Will there be any changes in procedure, perhaps because of expected turnout? Will there be unusual time limits on individual presentations, for example? Don't accept secondhand assurances. Call the chair—if not the chair, then the Council secretary or the City Attorney—nail it down and ask to be informed if things change.

While you're at it, ask how the Council will gauge support. Will folks be asked to stand in support and opposition? It's important to paper the room with our supporters anyway. But we still want to know how the Council will distinguish between property owners and others in attendance.

This is where we need to make our case for our petition. After all, it's easier for a nephew to stand with an uncle against us—regardless of what the Council requests—than for a nonresident owner who backs us to travel a great distance to be in attendance.

Finally, we'll want prior approval, if we need it, to make a unified presentation under the direction of our key presenter. If testimony is held to three to five minutes for each speaker, we want to know if we can put together a block of time among several speakers and then subdivide it as we see fit. The answer will determine how we plan and rehearse our presentation. We need absolute clarity here. It would be disastrous to begin and be ruled out of order.

When we do rise to be heard, we'll want to thank the chair for answering our questions and approving our format. This will remove any doubt in the minds of others about the propriety of what we're doing.

FORMATTING OUR DELIVERY

Now get with the steering committee and identify what you should cover. Decide who should speak on what issue, for how long and in what order.

Draw from your wider community of supporters to assure diversity and interest. Have each major group of supporters represented, but strive to keep the number of presenters limited. Four is good, six probably the maximum. Changing speakers takes time and requires listeners to adjust to the message. If you have a larger number of folks whose interests you think should be heard, consider having one speaker read one-sentence quotations as each rises in the audience. A retiree, for instance, may simply stand as you read her signed testimony (which you'll submit for the record), "I live on a limited income and believe the district is worth the price."

Get everyone together to discuss the plan and to draft very brief statements. Each presenter should rehearse his or her presentation in front of the others. Keep a stopwatch handy and play beat the clock. Practicing with others will help you find out whether what you think is good actually sounds good when spoken. If you just wait till the hearing, you'll run the risk of stopping to explain what you meant to say. That's like walking off a cliff, because you'll be a mess after that. But if you've practiced your presentation to perfection, then you'll have the confidence to say your piece and sit down.

Someone will have to be allocated a fair chunk of time to present our petition's results and explain our methodology. Use large pie charts for their visual effect, because most folks won't do the math in their heads.

Our position will be that the petition is stand-alone evidence of a popular majority for doing what the law and courts say is a legitimate activity. Even so, we may ask our supporters who are present to stand—but not be counted, because they have been counted already.

Be forward looking in your conclusion to underscore the compatibility of historic districting with community development and change. Once more stress the core of our civic vision, that we are taking responsibility for our future as well as our past.

We've been down that road so many times by now that you should be able to speak from your heart instead of from notes. And as FDR once advised, "Be sincere, be brief, be seated."

CAUTIONS

Bob Agee thinks this take-control approach will stand us in good stead. But he's also eager to share some cautionary perspectives from his experience. So we follow him back to his office for a chat.

> **Bob:** You want to be careful in several areas. When you get to the Council chamber, be aware that there may be personality conflicts up there between elected officials. Don't get caught up in their likes and don't-likes. Be dedicated and firm about your cause, but don't be overly defensive or irritated. Don't be impolite, rude, and obnoxious. Don't allow yourself to be pulled in and pulled down by someone else's lack of courtesy. Just extend courtesy even when it's not extended to you. At the end of the day, even if you can scream louder and scream more points at an elected official, that person *has* a vote and you *don't*. [Laughter.]

> **Me:** That seems commonsensical. We're going to work hard at presenting our case in a respectful and responsible manner.

Bob: But don't just assume people are working on a subject in good faith with the idea of trying to come up with a reasonable solution.

Me: [I give him my best interviewer's surprised well-why-not? look.]

Bob: Think about election cycles, for example. If members are wanting to get reelected, that can make everything different. Maybe someone is looking for an issue to make a campaign point, something to rally people around. So you may be in the unfortunate position of having a Council member who has decided to start a fire with the district issue—and pouring kerosene on it will help him get reelected. It might be that they want to keep someone else from getting elected. So they end up taking a position that has nothing to do with the subject matter of the issue. It just has to do with their own political survival in that case.

Me: Now you've got me thinking about the personality issue again. How should we be thinking about the interplay among Council members?

Bob: All of us have relationships with people we have confidence in. If a seatmate is expert in an area and I'm not, I might just follow her lead. The Council is just a group with the usual group dynamics. And there are people who are going to go against what someone else wants out of sheer spite. If the other guy is for it, they're against it. It's as simple as that.

Me: Which seems to caution against being identified too closely with the wrong official.

Bob: You want everybody's support. But another might then tell you, "I understand what you want. I don't have any problem with it. But you've got sponsor problems." That is, someone you might have as your champion is a pariah. The result is that you're encumbered that person's baggage. That's the unpleasant part of what is a dynamic political process.

Me: How can a political novice keep from blundering into that kind of political minefield?

Bob: Do your homework. If you don't know what to expect, you're already behind the eight ball and probably aren't going to get anywhere.

Me: Maybe we ought to hire a professional to handle the hearing for us. [Pause.] You don't look so sure. . . .

Bob: You have to be the judge of what you need. But I'd caution you to be careful that your speaker speaks to the right audience. I've seen it happen. You think they're going just a great job and you love everything they're saying. But up on the dais it's not going well with the Council members at all. What's happening is that your speaker is following his paycheck. He's talking to *you*, the audience that is *behind* him and not the audience that's going to make the decision. He—or she—doesn't need to convince *you*; they need to be convincing the *others*.

Me: And if we do it ourselves? Is there a secret to success?

Bob: Be firm but polite. You want to make it hard for them to dislike you. And don't forget to say "thank you." Say: "We really want to thank you for your interest and support on this. And at the conclusion, whichever way it goes, we appreciate your time." Politicians get blamed a lot. When you like the result, it's because the cause was good and it *should* have succeeded on its own merits. But if it doesn't go the way you want it to, then it's because "those people are dumb, incapable, and corrupt." The simple act of giving a little credit means a lot. It's probably the most powerful and underused weapon you have in getting where you're trying to go.

Me: But is that really going to win votes for us?

Bob: You don't want to lose votes. You have to know how to count. You need a majority. If you have eleven Council members, you need six. It's that simple. If you've got six or seven going in, you can feel great. But the only thing that's certain in politics is uncertainty. All of a sudden something comes up—a group from the audience surprises you. You look at the dais and see things are falling apart.

Me: Then what?

Bob: I have a saying: Never go into a room that doesn't have another door.

Me: Can we ask the Council for a postponement?

Bob: You can ask, but it doesn't mean you'll get it. The other side will object. Suppose you count seven votes before the hearing. Then one member comes down with the flu. That leaves you six. In the middle of the meeting another rushes out because of a family emergency. That's politics. If you're a general in the field and a general on the other side has something unfortunate happen, are you going to say, "Oh, give them a time-out!"? No. You're going to push the battle.

Me: So what kind of second door do you mean?

Bob: Remember the old saying: The perfect is the enemy of the possible. You might not be able to get 100 percent of what you want. Don't reject all amendments as hostile out of hand. Now, sometimes they *are* hostile. Sometimes they *are* meant to cripple. But don't be afraid to deal with amendments and take less than what you regard as the best. That's when you might get a delay, too. Thank them for bringing up "some good points." Say that you'd like to work on language with their staff that will satisfy their concerns. Still, if you have eight or nine votes you can count on, you can be less attentive and push things through.

Me: So how would you tell a friend to prepare for the hearing, to feel composed?

Bob: You mean you? *You* I'd tell, go have a good stiff drink and relax!

His smile said no hostility there, and I made sure to *thank* him for his help. We spoke briefly about the next chapter. I told him we'd be looking beyond tactical amendments to the far more serious question of responding to compromise pressures that might win the vote but gut our proposal. He gave me a look that said "good luck."

THIRTY-THREE

The Politics of Compromise

The middle of the road is for yellow lines and dead armadillos.

—Texas Representative Jim Hightower

And it's a long and winding road that brings us back to Newnan, Georgia, where we began. It's more a land of possums than armadillos, but the yellow lines are the same.

You remember Newnan, don't you? That's where the Planning and Zoning Department authored the fateful compromise that made their new design guidelines voluntary.

In the blink of an eye, Newnan got an unenforceable district on the books. "That's like making the speed limit voluntary," a critic said.[1] And guess who was left standing on the center line as politics sped over them? Yep, you've got it.

So our question is, just how can we get designation across the road so it isn't dead on arrival? We'll have to stop, look, and listen to keep from being blindsided by some last-minute compromise or concession aimed at winning Council approval.

WHERE WE STAND

Note: I said *last-minute.* The hour is late and the hearing has been difficult. After the wear and tear of our long campaign, do we still have it in us to stave off yet another assault on the district? As Nietzsche warned us, it is "when we are tired" that "we are attacked by ideas we conquered long ago."

So what old mental foe might be lying in wait for us now? Could it be an aversion to compromise that once marked us as political innocents? If we refuse to talk compromise here at the end, we'll be putting ourselves in harm's way with Council members.

But we're not that dumb. By now you and I both stand on the side of sound politics, that is for *firm principles vigorously defended* and *practical results resolutely pursued.* If the City Council wants to talk compromise, then fine. But let's do it on our terms and not those of our opponents.

WHAT OUR OPPONENTS WANT

When our adversaries talk compromise they advocate changes that amount to the same thing as no district at all. Their bottom line typically is that there needs to be "a way to opt out" of the district, as an opponent in Simpsonville, South Carolina, says.[2] But how? Their three most common solutions are:

- Exempt their properties—the so-called Swiss cheese option.

- Make the district's design review procedures voluntary.
- Let design review be mandatory, but compliance voluntary.

They all say the same thing politically: "Here's my compromise. I'll shut up about *your* district if I get to decide what I can do with *my* property."

THE PERIL OF LEGALISM

Each option raises a variety of legal issues for the Council. Nothing derails a hearing faster than legal uncertainties. So if any of these alternatives looks to figure in our hearing, you'll be wise to have a preservation law specialist ready to respond authoritatively. Talk with the City Attorney first, as well, so that the Council's own counsel is clear.

Being squared away on the law is important, but don't go getting legalistic on me. Don't rely on the law to extricate you from what is *right here, right now a political matter.* The City Council can pass any ordinance it wants, regardless of what anyone says the law is. And, sure, the courts might overturn it later. But that won't put us any closer to designation, and our political moment will have passed.

Legalism is the intellectual error of thinking that the law points the way for politics. Think instead of the flow going the other way. Let's take care of politics now, and sound, enduring law will follow.

DIAGRAMMING COMPROMISE

So where do we go with compromise? Most folks think that compromise is a matter of meeting each other halfway. Ask them to sketch out an issue and they'll draw a line with two opposed parties

breakers

Figure 33.1

at either end. Somewhere on that line—in the middle, they'll guess—lies the point of compromise.

Let's put it to the test. Take a look at the line below with the center line marked. I've placed the breakers—our inflexible can't-tell-me-what-to-do opponents—on the far right-hand end. Now write us in.

Do we go on the far left-hand side? We do only if we are equally inflexible save-it-at-all-costs preservationists. *But you and I are not on that end.*

Maybe we started out there a long time ago, but we know better now. We know that the legacy we cherish will have to find a future in communities that are livable, homes that are enjoyable, and businesses that are profitable. And we know that we don't get to define those terms. Property owners do.

We're practical preservationists. We've accommodated our vision to what our neighbors desire for themselves. We've already done just about all the compromising with them we practicably can, and we've produced a majority consensus for designation. Our coalition now occupies the vital center ground in our diagram. And that's right where we should be.

So we'll be happy to talk about compromise if that's what Council members want. But we'll talk about facts, not wishes. And our starting point will be: *the historic district* is *the compromise.*

HOW WE SEE COMPROMISE

That is an arresting claim. It should halt any headlong rush to find some—*any*—concession that'll paper over differences. We won't get much time to explain ourselves. Given a chance, I'd say something that more briefly tracks along like this:

1. The District as Our Compromise

I'd start by saying that the district is about far more than preservation. It's about forward-looking community development. It's an agreement we've negotiated with many of our neighbors who don't share our passion—the passion of preservationists—for our common historic legacy.

We ourselves would like to do more—perhaps a lot more—for preservation. But we've taken a "preservation-plus" approach. Through it we've fitted together a diverse group of personal and community interests that now support designation.

Our coalition's strength is seen in what each of us has given up. The district squeezes us as preservationists to work constructively with forces for change, and it squeezes those who advocate change to build upon the past. Its mandated procedures squeeze all of us as property owners, too. Yet each one of us for our own reasons has come to the conclusion that, as we say, "The juice is worth the squeeze."

And you know what? That's as fine an expression of how compromise works *when it works well* as you're likely to find anywhere. It's our opponents who have placed themselves beyond accommodation.

2. The District as Streaming Accommodation

Is it reasonable to ask the community to compromise this core compromise for the mere appearance—but not the substance—of agreement with breakers? No, of course not.

Compromising the district's arrangements will get us nowhere. And that's precisely where our opponents want it to go.

That's not surprising. The district will create a new political process for dealing with conflicting interests. It's always the case that such new arrangements are never welcomed by some of those whose interests get bigger play without them.

We're not singling out our opponents' interests, either. We've said from the beginning that everybody—including us—has interests that run into everybody else's all the time. When those conflicts affect the public interest, accommodations have to be found.

We're willing to work on our differences within a framework of guidelines and procedures. Our opponents are not. *We* talk about compromise and accommodation, and we put our money where our mouth is. *They* talk about compromise and they want to take a walk.

So what's the Council's responsibility? Is it to make the naysayers happy? Let's say it again: *of course not.* It is a fundamental axiom of democratic institutions that there only has to be enough majority interest to make them *possible*—while dissenting minority interest shows why they are *necessary*.

We on our side are agreed that our community needs a forum for a continuing conversation—*punctuated by authoritative decisions*—in which the community's interests in keeping historic resources in play will engage the widest array of other interests. That process may best be described as *streaming accommodation.*

LOOKING DOWN THE ROAD

Streaming accommodation. What does it mean?

It means that over, say, the next ten years scores of projects will be vetted through the HPC's procedures. Each review will aim at fitting preservation to the interests of the property owner and, conversely, the interests of the property owner to preservation. Each outcome, one after the other, will be a partial installment on our future.

Can't these arrangements be voluntary? Wouldn't that push the HPC to find accommodations rather than issue edicts? A good preservation commission will always work to get to "yes," but law is necessary. Without it, there will be no incentive for property owners to reciprocate. If the process fails, the Council can appoint new commissioners or revise the ordinance.

The district won't solve all our problems, nor is it intended to. Differences over teardowns and "McMansions," adaptive reuse and new construction, repair and replacement, traditional materials and new technologies will continue to confront us daily as our community evolves, pushed this way and that by competing interests. Yet that doesn't mean we shouldn't try to reach proximate settlements and, trying, find a practical way to move on down the road together.

IN THE COUNCIL'S INTEREST

So what's the Council's own interest in this? Its vote won't settle our differences with opponents. *But the vote will determine how and where those differences will be played out in the future.*

If we don't get the district, then we'll be back to fighting out our basic differences over and over, issue by issue, and project by project—and all without benefit of guidelines or ground rules. And guess where we'll be doing that!

I don't think I'd look forward to that prospect if I were on the City Council, would you? I'd much rather have the HPC play its role than to have the struggle over the future of the neighborhood dragged out before the Council again and again and again.

Council members shouldn't start down that road. But if they do, then now's the time to cross their path and stare them down. It won't be easy. It takes a tough bird to play chicken. But then every kid in the South knows why the chicken crossed the road. It was to show the possum it could be done.

NOTES

1. Kevin Duffy, "History a Matter of Heart in Newnan," www.ajc.com, *Atlanta Constitution-Journal*, June 9, 2003.

2. April M. Silvaggio, "Debate Heats Up over Simpsonville District," www.greenville.com, *Greenville News*, August 8, 2004.

THIRTY-FOUR

Winning the Vote

Rommel, you magnificent bastard! I read your book!

—George C. Scott, *Patton*

The scene was General George S. Patton's opening clash with Field Marshal Erwin Rommel's panzers in North Africa. As Patton crushed his enemy he acknowledged that Rommel's prewar writings had given him the key to the U.S. Army's first armored victory in World War II.

As I've written this primer, I've kept Patton's words in mind. There is always a chance that our opponents will read our book and see our strategy.

Generally speaking—if you'll forgive my pun—I doubt you'll run into any Pattons in your neighborhood. Still, you never know. But even if you do, and they gain some advantage here or there, we'll be better off for having had this discussion among ourselves.

Still, some things are better passed over in silence. And that brings me to my conclusion.

DO THE UNEXPECTED

There are currents in all politics that sometimes carry us forward and sometimes pull against us. That's why successful action always depends upon partial readings of swiftly moving contingencies.

And so it is that our strategic line might not be sufficient to win the vote for designation. I want to prepare you for that eventuality, too.

I want you to think *outside the box* and prepare to do the unexpected. Be brilliant! Catch your opponents off guard, move the Council, and win the district that your community needs.

I could, perhaps, point you in the right direction. But it wouldn't be smart to lay all our cards on the table, now would it? I think it's best to leave our final stroke to your own imagination and cunning.

THE STEADY FLOW OF POLITICS

And now at last congratulations all round! The vote is in. We've won the district. "So," as Othello said, "they laugh that win."

What's next for us? Do we follow the lead of Cincinnatus, the Roman citizen-politician, and return to our plow now that the public's work is done?

Not on your life, unless you want to give our opponents the last laugh. Politics is a continuously flowing river. It was already well along when we waded into it in chapter 3, and it won't stop now.

Is this so difficult to see? I trust not. But if you thought that politics began when you first proposed the district, then you might be inclined to think it will cease with designation.

So tell me. Were you looking forward to leaving the rough-and-tumble of the political contest for the more settled, civilized business of the district's administration? If you were, then you're about to learn that administering the district is just a continuation of politics by other means.

As I started this book, I met Bettie L. Kerr at the NAPC's 2004 Forum in Indianapolis. She is the Historic Preservation Officer for the Lexington Fayette Urban County Government in Kentucky. "Anybody who does preservation and doesn't know he's a politician," she told me, "is making a mistake."

Well, now, I guess that makes you a politician, doesn't it? You've already run a campaign and made promises. It's time you kept them. So get yourself back down to City Hall, see the Mayor, and offer to serve on the HPC. The district is going to need your leadership in our community.

Heaven knows, you've already been sworn *at*. Now step up, raise your right hand, and be sworn in.

$\mathcal{I}_{n} de x$

Mesa, Arizona, 139
Michigan, 7, 37, 39, 89, 147,
  180
Missoula, Montana, 221
Mona Lisa, 201
money, 27, 70, 71, 142, 148, 150,
  166, 230
Montana, 221
moral high ground, 91
morality of winning, 12, 80
Morris, Dick, 44, 212, 235

NAPC. *See* National Alliance of
  Preservation Commissions
National Alliance of Historic
  Commissions (NAPC), 3, 13,
  256
national historic districts. *See*
  historic districts
National Register, 25–26
National Trust for Historic
  Preservation, 3, 13, 139, 161
negotiating with breakers: politics
  of, 182–83; rules, 184; venues,
  184–85
Nevada, 9
New Mexico, 9, 59
New Orleans, Louisiana, 19
Newnan, Georgia, 6, 142, 246
newspaper. *See* press
Newton, Massachusetts, 179
New York, 6, 91, 151
New York City, New York, 151
Nietzsche, Friedrich, 247
NIMBY, 210
North Carolina, 139

Oak Ridge, North Carolina, 1–2,
  25, 79–81, 36–40, 51, 79–81,
  83, 139, 157
O'Conner, Maggie, 25–35, 37, 38,
  40, 83
O'Neill, Thomas Phillip "Tip,"
  Jr., 11
opinion, public. *See* public
  opinion
opponents. *See* breakers
Orange, California, 19
Othello, 255
overlay historic district. *See*
  historic district

Palo Alto, California, 6
partnership: with City planners,
  30, 41; with local preservation
  organizations, 68, 70–72
patriotism, abuse of, 162
Patton, George S., 254
Pennsylvania, 7, 22, 138
personal attacks, 87–92
petition, 17, 171–81, 205, 215,
  223, 239; circulating, 106–7;
  counting signatures, 178–79;
  cyber, 176; drafting, 172–74;
  exclusions, 174–75; mail-in
  survey, 177; model petition,
  174; in public hearings,
  240–41; securing signatures,
  175–77; statistics as politics,
  179–81; submitting, 177–78;
  who signs, 171–72
Philadelphia, Pennsylvania, 7, 22,
  138

About the Author

Bill Schmickle chairs the Historic Preservation Commission in Annapolis, Maryland. He was a cofounder of the Oak Ridge Historic District in North Carolina. He and his wife, Charlotte, own and operate Flag House Inn in the Annapolis Historic District (www.flaghouseinn.com). A former professor of politics, he writes and consults on preservation (www.preservationpolitics.com).